SERMON IN A SENTENCE

St. Teresa of Avila

SERMON IN A SENTENCE

*A Treasury of Quotations
on the Spiritual Life*

FROM THE WRITINGS OF

St. Teresa of Avila

DOCTOR OF THE CHURCH

*Arranged according to the Virtues of
the Holy Rosary
and Other Spiritual Topics*

Selected and Arranged by
JOHN P. McCLERNON

IGNATIUS PRESS   SAN FRANCISCO

Cover art by Christopher J. Pelicano
Cover design by Roxanne Mei Lum

Frontispiece by Edith Beckwith Smith
Combermere, Ontario, Canada

© 2005 Ignatius Press, San Francisco
All rights reserved
ISBN 978-1-58617-089-9
ISBN 1-58617-089-9
Library of Congress Control Number 2005926546
Printed in the United States of America ∞

It is a great good to think that if we try we can become saints with God's help. And have no fear that He will fail if we don't fail. Since we have not come here for any other thing, let us put our hands to the task.

—St. Teresa of Avila

DEDICATION

This volume in the "Sermon in a Sentence" series is dedicated, as are all these works, to my loving wife, Mary, and to the five beautiful children with whom God has blessed our marriage: Christopher, Clare, Catherine, David, and Stephen.

I also wish to make note of the invaluable assistance and advice given once again by my mother, Judy McClernon. She is a Secular Carmelite, and in so many aspects a true daughter of St. Teresa of Avila. It was above all the writings and teachings of this great saint that led my mother to the Third Order of the Discalced Carmelites so many years ago.

Last of all, but certainly not least, I wish to thank St. Teresa of Avila for all these treasured quotes and short sayings on the spiritual life. It is she who is the real author of this book. I consider it a great privilege to be an instrument in bringing her writings to you.

CONTENTS

OTHER TOPICS

FOREWORD

I have been a great admirer of the sixteenth-century Spanish mystics and Doctors of the Church St. Teresa of Jesus (known as St. Teresa of Avila) and St. John of the Cross. The passion with which they love the Lord and the wholehearted gift of "self" to Him in His service is something that pulls at the human heart. They have found the Answer to all, they have encountered the Totally Other Who makes us whole in the person of Jesus Christ our Lord, and they call out to the world to follow in their footsteps. They invite us to become the person that God desires us to be—they urge and inspire us to wholeness, to holiness.

Since entering the Order of the Discalced Carmelites in 1983, I have always found the writings of our holy parents, St. Teresa of Jesus and St. John of the Cross, fresh, significant, and valid for our postmodern world. The questions that haunt modern man are the same questions that have haunted mankind throughout its history— the desire for completeness seems to elude its grasp because mankind has tried to fashion the answer for itself. Mankind is still enthralled with itself, with its capacity to invent, to solve, to control. The great St. Teresa calls mankind out of this self-absorbed illusion and invites us to enter into a life-giving significant friendship with the Lord Jesus. It is in this genuine, living, dynamic relationship that we find our fulfillment. Fulfillment is encountered in love; it cannot be manufactured or forced: it is the fruit of love and self-surrender.

Teresa is not a dreamy-eyed romantic; she is a passionate
realist. She knows the difficult task that she invites us
into, but she also has experienced the fruits of this task
and knows that they far supercede any of the difficulties
of self-surrender. She knows our capacity for self-deceit
and self-denial—she asks for accountability as she ushers
us into the presence of the compassionate Truth.

I applaud Mr. John McClernon for his prodigious work.
I have read and reread this book. I have taken it with me
to prayer and have listened to the voice of Teresa, full of
the inspiration of the Holy Spirit. It is my prayer that
the general public will take advantage of the treasure
chest that is offered here in these pages. Mr. McClernon
has demonstrated his love for St. Teresa through this hard
work of gathering together many of the nuggets of wisdom of this mystic. They are now offered to you for
your enjoyment and inspiration.

Father Stephen Sanchez, O.C.D.
Mt. Carmel Center
Dallas, Texas

INTRODUCTION

There are many Catholics who would like nothing better than to read the actual writings of the Church's spiritual giants. But how many do? The culture of today leads one to embrace such a busy lifestyle. All too often the time needed to feed the soul takes a back seat, and one ends up spiritually starved. *Sermon in a Sentence* is designed for just such a person.

Imagine spending a few minutes with St. Teresa of Avila, a Doctor of the Church and rightfully considered one of the greatest mystics in the history of Christianity. Many saints over the last four hundred-plus years have confidently followed the spiritual advice and insight found in her writings, and even today souls seeking perfection and a deep love of Christ continue to find in her a beacon of light, leading them to a genuine, deep, and holy way of life. Whether you consider yourself a beginner or advanced in the spiritual life, following her advice and wisdom will certainly lead you ever deeper to the heart of God. This book has been designed to bring the inspiration of her words to you in a very simple and direct format.

Hundreds of quotations and short sayings taken from the writings of St. Teresa of Avila have been classified by the Christian virtues of which they speak and then arranged to complement the fifteen-decade Rosary, proceeding from the first joyful mystery (the Annunciation, with its

virtue of humility) to the fifth glorious mystery (the
Crowning of Mary, with its virtue of devotion to Mary).
For those who choose to use these excerpts for meditation while reciting the Rosary, we have placed a type
ornament after the tenth one, to mark the end of a decade.
Additional quotations follow, for use with a Rosary or
for separate meditation. A selection of quotations on other
spiritual topics of interest follows, bringing the reader a
sample of St. Teresa's insights into subjects such as prayer,
the Eucharist, the Church, and family life.

It is hoped that this little book will serve as an effective
introduction to one of our world's greatest spiritual mas-
ters. May these quotes and short sayings find a place in
your heart and soul and draw you closer to our Lord
Jesus Christ, Whom St. Teresa loved and served so well.

ACKNOWLEDGMENTS

The author is grateful for permission granted by the Institute of Carmelite Studies, Washington, D.C., to use extracts from the following volumes:

The Collected Works of St. Teresa of Avila. Volume 1. Translated by Kieran Kavanaugh, O.C.D. and Otilio Rodriguez, O.C.D. Washington, D.C.: Institute of Carmelite Studies, 1976.

The Collected Works of St. Teresa of Avila. Volume 2. Translated by Kieran Kavanaugh, O.C.D. and Otilio Rodriguez, O.C.D. Washington, D.C.: Institute of Carmelite Studies, 1980.

The Collected Works of St. Teresa of Avila. Volume 3. Translated by Kieran Kavanaugh, O.C.D. and Otilio Rodriguez, O.C.D. Washington, D.C.: Institute of Carmelite Studies, 1985.

In the text of this book, the references are indicated by volume number, followed by a colon and then by the page number. For example, 1:31 indicates that the extract is from volume 1, page 31.

St. Teresa of Avila

(1515–1582)

Doctor of the Church

Virgin and Foundress of the Discalced Carmelites

This sixteenth-century contemplative nun's spiritual insights and reflections on the soul's union with Jesus Christ—coupled and flavored with her unique gifts of charm, humor, and common sense—have made her one of the greatest mystics and spiritual directors in the history of Christianity. St. Teresa of Avila has left in her wake a treasury of writings and teachings on the spiritual life; she has blazed a trail that marks the profound, mystical, and loving union that she experienced with our Lord. The unique experiences and practical wisdom of St. Teresa of Avila cover all aspects of the spiritual life, notably prayer and the action of God's grace in a human soul. She was certainly a uniquely blessed soul who was destined by God to impart to His children of all walks of life the ways of holiness and sanctity. Teresa's courageous efforts and steadfast love of God in the midst of seemingly countless obstacles has provided inspiration and example for many a saint after her. Once she gave her heart fully to Jesus Christ, there was nothing to keep her from reaching the heights of mystical prayer. She boldly pursued His holy will for her, both within and without the cloister walls of a Carmelite convent. She once said, "Always have courageous thoughts. As a result of them the Lord will give you grace for courageous deeds. . . . These brave thoughts are important." This saintly woman speaks to all, regardless of one's vocation in life. She speaks clearly and authoritatively as a true daughter of the Church. For professional, cleric, workman, home-maker, or nun—St. Teresa's wisdom is as fresh and timely today as it was in medieval Spain. Over four hundred years after her death, the Church continues to be blessed by the great Order of the Discalced Carmelites, who stand as an eternal tribute to the vision and inspiration of a great foundress, pioneer, and lover of God.

Teresa was born of a noble family in Avila, Spain, on March 28, 1515, in the home of Don Alfonso and Dona Beatriz Capeda. The Capeda family was a large one, Teresa being the third of nine children born in this marriage—the second marriage for Don Alfonso, who earlier had been left widowed with three children. Her mother and father were both very pious Catholics and reared their children in the ways of God and His Church. As a young child, Teresa was unusually active, imagina-tive, and sensitive. Religious thought and influences were very strong in her life, and even at a young age she was fascinated by stories of the saints and martyrs. A charm-ing account of this took place when Teresa was seven years old. The pious young girl and her closest brother, Rodrigo, decided that the best and quickest way to heaven was to be a martyr for Christ. They set out discreetly from home one day, planning to beg as Franciscans all the way to Africa, where their goal was to be martyred for the faith. God had other plans though, and this early undertaking was thwarted by an uncle who found the two children and brought them home.

At the age of fourteen a dramatic change in Teresa's life began not long after she experienced the untimely death of her mother. Teresa, who was always fond of books, turned her avid reading obsession to the worldly popular romances of her day. The pious practices of her youth would soon fall by the wayside, to be replaced with tales of chivalry, knights and ladies, jousts, and foolish loves. Her father noticed this change of heart and decided to place Teresa in a Benedictine convent school where other young girls of her social class were being educated. She was to remain there for a year and a half, only to be brought back to her family home due to a deteriorating health condition.

When she eventually recovered, Teresa was sent out to the countryside in order to live with one of her sisters. It was during this time that she started to consider religious life and rekindle a love of God. Feeling unworthy and seeking direction, she turned to the intercession of St. Mary Magdalen and St. Augustine and began reading the Letters of St. Jerome. Her subsequent decision to enter the Carmelite monastery in Avila was initially opposed by her father, who wanted his daughter to wait until he had passed away. Teresa, however, felt that a delay in her plans to be a nun would weaken her resolve. Face to face with one of the most difficult decisions in her life, one day she discreetly left home for the Carmelite convent just outside of Avila, where a close friend of hers was already living, and she applied for admission. Teresa made her profession there a year later.

Once again a serious illness would result in her being removed from the convent and returning home for recovery. This time Teresa's recovery would be marked by intense suffering, reducing her to almost complete paralysis. She was at one time even given up for dead. But a gradual improvement in health took place, which Teresa credited to the prayer of St. Joseph, whose powerful intercession she would advocate the rest of her life.

Our Lord used this time in Teresa's life to lead her to a deeper, contemplative prayer life with Him. She began to concentrate on mental prayer and progress in the ways of spiritual perfection. Her return to the Carmelite convent after a three-year absence, however, brought her ideals of sanctity to a halt, due to the many distractions there that hindered, rather than provided, an environment conducive to a devout contemplative life of prayer and union with Christ. At that time many of the convents in Spain had become more like homes for single women who had little or no true aspirations to live a cloistered religious life. The convent in Avila allowed continuous visitors, socializing, gossip, and privileges contrary to the original Carmelite rule of life. Teresa's intelligence, charm, and witty nature fell right into this worldly atmosphere, and she eventually neglected the practice of mental prayer. The Lord continued to call her back to Him, and in 1553 she experienced a conversion of heart while meditating upon an image of Christ Crucified. Pondering the Suffering Servant, Teresa realized how much He loved her and how little she had returned that love to Him. She vowed at that moment to cease all self-interest and irreligious practices.

This conversion was lasting and permanent. Never again would weariness, poor health, or opposition hold back Teresa in the spiritual life. She plunged her soul into a deeper life of prayer and contemplation, and the Lord blessed her with many mystical visions, raptures, inner voices, and heavenly visitations. Teresa scaled the heights of mysticism, and today she is regarded as one of

the greatest Christian contemplatives. The key to open-
ing the doors to the grace and power of God is a very
close, intimate friendship with Him. This personal and
continual union with Christ is based on a solid life of
prayer and sacrifice. She tells us: "Prayer is the door to
favors as great as those He granted me. If this door is
closed, I don't know how He will grant them. . . . It seems
to me in this life there could be no greater good than
the practice of prayer."

Teresa soon realized that a complete reform was needed
in order to live the authentic spirit of Carmel, so she
embraced a bold plan to reform the Carmelite Order
and bring it back to its true monastic roots. Her first few
years championing this effort demanded heroic endur-
ance on the part of the idealistic nun, who suffered much
from people around her. Almost everyone within and
without the convent disapproved of her disciplined life
of prayer, penances, and absolute adherence to the ancient
Carmelite rule. In the midst of so much persecution and
slander God continued to bless Teresa with His sweet-
ness and mystical consolations. She was sometimes seen
lifted from the ground in sheer ecstacy, and she experienced the rare privilege of a mystical marriage with
Christ. Once an angel appeared by her side and pierced
her heart with a heavenly lance, which she later claimed
"left me wholly on fire with a great love of God".

St. Peter of Alcantara, a holy Franciscan priest with
noted experience on the inner life, would champion Teresa's cause. While other nuns, confessors, and prelates
misunderstood and opposed Teresa, St. Peter noticed the
unmistakable signs of the Holy Spirit that were empow-
ering her life. He also predicted further tribulations for
the courageous nun.

Teresa was a friend and confidant of two others who would be canonized saints: Francis Borgia, a Jesuit, and John of the Cross, a Carmelite who would follow her lead by reforming the contemplative men of the Order. Teresa's courage and steadfast faith were unshakable and firm despite the difficulties she encountered. "Never despair", she said, "or fail to trust in the greatness of God."

Reluctantly and out of obedience to her confessors, Teresa began to write down her experiences and practical advice on the spiritual life, union with God, and the inner workings of grace in the soul. One can discern in her writings no self-love or pride, but rather forgiveness toward those who persecuted her. Some of the most breathtaking, yet practical spiritual advice flowed from the pen of this enlightened Carmelite nun, especially during the last fifteen years of her life, when God called Teresa to engage actively in the founding of new convents of reformed Carmelites. These writings are spiritual masterpieces and even today inspire souls desirous of pursuing a deep spiritual life. She writes with authority on all aspects of the spiritual life. Foremost among these writings are the well-known *Way of Perfection* (guidance for her nuns), *Foundations* (an account of her work in founding new monasteries), and *Interior Castle* (a title given by Christ Himself). *Interior Castle* is considered by many as her greatest work. It was for her profound knowledge on the mystical life and union with Christ along with those of her Carmelite contemporary St. John of the Cross that later earned each of them the honorary title of "Doctor of the Church".

With heavenly inspiration, the approval of the Carmelite provincial, and Peter of Alcantara's prayers and

encouragement, Teresa engaged in the task of establish-
ing new Carmelite convents that followed a stricter, more
contemplative way of life. Although she was in her late
forties at this time and dealing with continued frail health,
Teresa's greatest accomplishments still lay ahead. The first
new convent, named after St. Joseph, was a small one in
Avila, consisting of four novices who were willing to
follow Teresa's lead. Her spiritual and temporal struggles
in founding this convent and those that followed, with
both secular and Church authorities (not to mention
those within her own order), are well documented in
the book *Foundations*. It is truly a remarkable work of
God how one of the greatest mystics in the history of
Christianity was also so keenly adept in dealing with
people from all walks of life. Local lay people, build-
ing contractors, attorneys, magistrates, and Church
officials—many of whom provided formidable obstacles
to her plans—could only hinder, but not stop the work
of God through this holy nun. Teresa's illnesses continued to baffle the physicians of her time, and it was by
sheer willpower, heroic determination, and unbounded
faith in God that she continued to scale the heights of
mysticism while still remaining a shrewd business-
woman, capable administrator, counselor, and foundress.

Teresa eventually won over the obstinate and unyield-
ing with her practical wisdom, charm, humility, and sense
of humor. She personally guided and taught her nuns all
aspects of a true monastic life and governed them with
great humility and charity. The Lord blessed these
reformed Carmelite foundations with many holy women.
It is interesting to note that this great foundress looked
more for intelligence, good humor, and common sense,
rather than piety, when selecting novices. "Heaven

preserve me", she once said, "from sullen saints." On one noted occasion when her nuns found Teresa in ecstacy, holding the Christ child in her arms, they followed her through the convent halls, singing and dancing.

The last fifteen years of Teresa's life brought many travels, mostly within Spain. During this interval of her life Teresa was called on to establish new foundations, while visiting others and dealing with many Church and secular authorities. At the age of sixty-five and in broken health, sheer willpower and the grace of God kept her alive; during the last two years of her life, Teresa still found the strength to establish three more convents. The Church would be blessed with sixteen reformed Carmelite convents before Teresa's work on earth was finished. That's an amazing feat, considering her poor health and the hardships of travel by mule-drawn carts and carriages throughout some of Spain's poorest and most dangerous roads, over mountains, rivers, and dry plains. Rude lodgings and scant food were daily occurrences.

In October 1582, even though feeling ill, Teresa set out to visit one of her convents. Her sickness got worse while traveling in an area which provided few if any places to stop. When she finally arrived at the convent, she was immediately put to bed due to her state of physical exhaustion. She did not recover from this illness. Her love of Jesus knew no bounds, and death was viewed by Teresa, as it was by so many saints before and after her, as something not to be feared, but as the final gateway to an eternity with God. "I die", she had once written years before, "because I do not die." As death approached and she received the Sacrament of the Anointing of the Sick and the Eucharist, she sat up and said, "O my Lord, now is the time that we shall see each other!" and then she passed away.

St. Teresa of Avila has been and continues to be one of the most popular and loved saints in the history of Christianity. The Discalced Carmelites today remain one of the great contemplative orders of the Catholic Church. Many aspiring men and women are drawn to a way of life and prayer that, if not pioneered, then was certainly reaffirmed, by the life of this great Spanish mystic. In 1622 Teresa was canonized a saint by the Catholic Church. Over three hundred years later, in 1970, she and St. Catherine of Siena were declared "Doctors of the Church" by Pope Paul VI. These saints were the first women on whom this great honor was conferred.

"The more that love and humility grow, the greater the fragrance these flowers of virtues give off, both for oneself and for others."

—St. Teresa of Avila

THE
JOYFUL
MYSTERIES

The First Joyful Mystery

The Annunciation of Our Lord

Humility

Whoever humbles himself like this child, he is the greatest in the kingdom of heaven.—Matthew 18:4

Without God nothing is accomplished. (1:106)

Let us understand most clearly the real fact: God gives [gifts] to us without any merit on our part. And let us thank His Majesty for them, because, if we do not acknowledge we are receiving them, we will not awaken ourselves to love. (1:106)

Love is the genuine fruit of prayer when prayer is rooted in humility. (1:107)

Humility has an excellent feature: when it is present in a work, that work does not leave in the soul a feeling of frustration. (1:122)

I am certain the Lord would not allow any harm to come to someone who strives humbly to reach Him. (1:122–23)

Let humility always go first so as to understand that this strength does not come from ourselves. (1:124)

This path of self knowledge must never be abandoned, nor is there on this journey a soul so much a giant that it has no need to return often to the stage of an infant and a suckling. And this should never be forgotten. (1:129–30)

There is no stage of prayer so sublime that it isn't necessary to return often to the beginning. Along this path of prayer, self knowledge and the thought of one's sins is the bread with which all palates must be fed no matter how delicate they may be; they cannot be sustained without this bread. (1:130)

Believe me, in the presence of infinite Wisdom, a little study of humility and one act of humility is worth more than all the knowledge of the world. (1:143)

My experience explains—and close attention should be given to it for the love of the Lord—that even though a soul may reach the stage in which God grants it such wonderful favors in prayer, it should not trust in itself; it can fall. Nor should it in any way place itself in the occasions of falling. (1:170)

❦

What I have come to understand is that this whole groundwork of prayer is based on humility and that the more a soul lowers itself in prayer the more God raises it up. (1:196)

If His Majesty should desire to raise us to the position of one who is an intimate and shares His secrets, we ought to accept gladly; if not, we ought to serve in the humbler tasks and not sit down in the best place.... God is more careful than we are, and He knows what is fitting for each one. (1:197)

It is a dangerous thing to be satisfied with ourselves. (1:279)

True humility doesn't come to the soul with agitation or disturbance, nor does it darken it or bring it dryness. Rather, true humility consoles and acts in a completely opposite way: quietly, gently, and with light. (1:257)

The Lord taught me this truth: that I should be determined and certain that His favor was not some good thing belonging to me but that it belonged to God; that just as I wasn't sorry to hear other persons praised ..., I should neither be sorry that His works be shown in me. (1:270)

I do not call "giving up everything" entering religious life, and the perfect soul can be detached and humble anywhere. (2:30)

Humility does not disturb or disquiet however great it may be; it comes with peace, delight, and calm.... The

pain of genuine humility doesn't agitate or afflict the
soul; rather, this humility expands it and enables it to
serve God more. (2:31)

Oh, my Sisters, do not feel secure or let yourselves go
to sleep! By feeling secure you would resemble someone who very tranquilly lies down after having locked
his doors for fear of thieves while allowing the thieves to
remain inside the house. . . . There is no worse thief than
we ourselves. (2:76)

Humility and mortification . . . were so much praised
by the King of Glory and so confirmed by His many
trials. Now, my daughters, this is the work that must be
done in order to escape from the land of Egypt, for in
finding these virtues you will find the manna. All things
will taste good to you. (2:77)

Believe me in one thing: if there is any vain esteem of
honor or wealth . . . you will never grow very much or
come to enjoy the true fruit of prayer. (2:83)

Let each one consider how much humility she has, and
she will see what progress has been made. (2:84)

Clearly, a humble person will reflect on his life and consider how he has served the Lord in comparison with
how the Lord ought to be served and the wonders the
Lord performed in lowering Himself so as to give us an
example of humility. (2:84)

I see that not making excuses for oneself is a habit characteristic of high perfection, and very meritorious; it gives great edification. (2:90)

There's no queen like humility for making the King surrender. Humility drew the King from heaven to the womb of the Virgin. (2:94)

And realize that the one who has more humility will be the one who possesses Him more; and the one who has less will possess Him less. For I cannot understand how there could be humility without love or love without humility. (2:94)

Let [us] consider how true humility consists very much in great readiness to be content with whatever the Lord may want to do with [us]. . . . If contemplating, practicing mental and vocal prayer, taking care of the sick, helping with household chores, and working even at the lowliest tasks are all ways of serving the Guest who comes to be with us . . . what difference does it make whether we serve in one way or the other? (2:101)

The angels who assist Him know well the attitude of their King, for He delights more in the unpolished manners of a humble shepherd who He realizes would say more if he knew more than He does in the talk of very wise and learned men, however elegant their discourse, if they don't walk in humility. (2:123)

Only humility can do something, a humility not acquired by the intellect, but by a clear perception that comprehends in a moment the truth ... about what a trifle we are and how very great God is. (2:165)

I give you one counsel: that you don't think that through your own strength or efforts you can arrive. ... But with simplicity and humility, which will achieve everything. (2:165)

Oh, by how many things was I offended! I am ashamed now. ... I didn't consider or pay any heed to the honor that is beneficial; that is, the honor that benefits the soul. (2:178)

The truly humble person always walks in doubt about his own virtues, and usually those he sees in his neighbors seem more certain and more valuable. (2:188)

The devil's aim is to make us think we are humble and, in turn, if possible, make us lose confidence in God. When you find yourselves in this condition, stop thinking about your misery, insofar as possible, and turn your thoughts to the mercy of God. (2:189–90)

The devil sets up another dangerous temptation: self-assurance in the thought that we will in no way return to our past faults and worldly pleasures. ... With it a person doesn't care against entering once more into the occasions of sin, and he falls. (2:190)

Remember your sins, and if in some matters people speak the truth in praising you, note that the virtue is not yours and that you are obliged to serve more. (2:227)

Self-knowledge and humility grow as the soul moves onward. (2:270)

I wouldn't want any relaxation ever in this regard, however high you may have climbed into the heavens. While we are on this earth nothing is more important to us than humility. (2:292)

Be convinced that where humility is truly present God will give a peace and conformity—even though He may never give consolations—by which one will walk with greater contentment than will others with their consolations. (2:308-9)

Humility is the ointment for our wounds because if we indeed have humility, even though there may be a time of delay, the surgeon, who is our Lord, will come to heal us. (2:311)

If souls are humble they will be moved to give thanks. If there is some lack in humility, they will feel an inner distaste for which they will find no reason. (2:313)

Humility! humility! By this means the Lord allows Himself to be conquered with regard to anything we want from Him. (2:326)

I understand that the Lord leaves [the soul] to its own
human nature for its own greater good. It then sees that
if it had been able to do something, the power was given
by His Majesty. (2:393)

I consider one day of humble self-knowledge a greater
favor from the Lord, even though the day may have cost
us numerous afflictions and trials, than many days of
prayer. (3:123)

Of all that He blesses you, a humble spirit is the best.
                                                    (3:406)

The Second Joyful Mystery

The Visitation to Elizabeth

Love of Neighbor

You shall love your neighbor as yourself.
—Mark 12:31

I saw some new virtues arise in me . . . not speaking evil of anyone, no matter how slight, but ordinarily avoiding all fault-finding. I was very much aware that I should not desire to say of another person what I would not want them to say of me. I was extremely cautious about this. (1:77–78)

If through my intercession I could play a part in getting a soul to love and praise God more, even if it be for just a short time, I think that would matter more to me than being in glory. (1:438)

Whoever fails to love their neighbor, fails to love You, my Lord, since we see You showed the very great love You have for the children of Adam by shedding so much blood. (1:445)

Let us strive always to look at the virtues and good deeds we see in others and cover their defects with the thought of our own great sins. (1:127)

While we live in this mortal life, earthly joys are uncertain, even when they seem to be given by You, if they are not accompanied by love of neighbor. (1:444–45)

For at times it happens that some trifle will cause as much suffering to one as a great trial will to another; little things can bring much distress to persons who have sensitive natures. If you are not like them, do not fail to be compassionate. (2:30)

Do not be negligent about showing gratitude. (2:47)

What would it matter were I to remain in purgatory until judgment day if through my prayer I could save even one soul? How much less would it matter if my prayer is to the advantage of many and for the honor of the Lord. (2:50)

It is most important that we have this [love for one another], for there is nothing annoying that is not suffered easily by those who love one another.... If this commandment were observed in the world as it should be, I think such love would be very helpful for the observance of the other commandments. (2:54)

[A] good means to having God is to speak with His friends, for one always gains very much from this.... I was always very attached to their praying for me, and so I strove to get them to do this. (2:67)

Oh, how good and true will be the love of the Sister who can help others by setting aside her own advantage for their sake. She will make much progress in all the virtues.... Better friendship will this be than all the tender words that can be uttered. (2:69)

Another very good proof of love is that you strive in household duties to relieve others of work. (2:70)

Help one another. This is the practice in which each one should strive to be ahead of the others. (2:83)

If a person is able ... he will serve God more and enlighten some soul that would have been lost, and ... by serving more he will merit the capacity to enjoy God more. (2:112)

Let truth dwell in your hearts, as it should through meditation, and you will see clearly the kind of love we are obliged to have for our neighbor. (2:115)

He said only, "forgive us because we forgive." ... To be forgiving is a virtue difficult for us to attain by ourselves but most pleasing to His Father. (2:180)

This is what we must strive for earnestly, to be affable, agreeable, and pleasing to persons with whom we deal. (2:200)

And when you have to suffer something for our Lord or for your neighbor, do not be afraid of your sins. You could perform one of these works with so much charity that all your sins would be pardoned. (2:239)

One must not place limits on a Lord so great and desirous to grant favors.... When they are from God the virtues grow so strong and love becomes so enkindled that there's no concealing the two. Even without any specific desire on the part of the soul, they always bring profit to other souls. (2:255)

It seems to me that one of the greatest consolations a person can have on earth must be to see other souls helped through his own efforts. (2:258)

Mutual love is so important that I would never want it to be forgotten. The soul could lose its peace and even disturb the peace of others by going about looking at trifling things in people. (2:296)

In this house, glory to God, there's not much occasion for gossip ... but it is good that we be on guard. (2:296)

Briefly, in all things we have to let God be the judge. (2:307)

Let us look at our own faults and leave aside those of others, for it is very characteristic of persons with such well-ordered lives to be shocked by everything. (2:315)

The more advanced you see you are in love for your neighbor the more advanced you will be in the love of God. (2:351)

The love His Majesty has for us is so great that to repay us for our love of neighbor He will in a thousand ways increase the love we have for Him. I cannot doubt this. (2:351)

I see, Sisters, that if we fail in our love of neighbor we are lost. (2:353)

Try to play a part in getting even one soul to praise God more. (2:392)

When, daughters, will we imitate this great God? . . . We should very eagerly endure everything, and let us love the one who offends us since this great God has not ceased to love us even though we have offended Him very much. (2:419)

Let us take special care, Sisters, to beg this mercy of Him and not be careless, for it is a most generous alms to pray for those who are in mortal sin. (2:429)

Well, then, what if through your prayer the chains could be loosed? The answer is obvious. For the love of God I ask you always to remember in your prayers souls in mortal sin. (2:429)

Apart from the fact that by prayer you will be helping greatly, you need not be desiring to benefit the whole world but must concentrate on those who are in your company, and thus your deed will be greater since you are more obliged toward them. (2:449)

This is the inclination the Lord has given me, for it seems to me that He prizes a soul that through our diligence and prayer we gain for Him, through His mercy, more than all the services we can render Him. (3:102)

I hold that our Lord never grants so great a favor to a person without allowing others to share in it as well. (3:211)

My desire is always to be some means by which our Lord may be praised and that there be more to serve Him. (3:256)

The Third Joyful Mystery

The Birth of Jesus

Spirit of Poverty

> *Blessed are the poor in spirit, for theirs is the kingdom of heaven.*—Matthew 5:3

I had the light that made everything coming to an end seem of little value to me, and it made those goods that can be gained by the love of God seem of great value since they are eternal. (1:70)

Serve God and reflect on how all things come to an end. (1:89)

We have our attachments since we do not strive to direct our desires to a good effect and raise them up from the earth completely; but to have many spiritual consolations along with attachments is incongruous, nor does it seem to me that the two can get along together. (1:111)

Those who in fact risk all for God will find that they have both lost all and gained all. (1:151)

43

If with money I could have bought the good I now see in myself, I would have esteemed it highly. . . . What is it we buy with this money we desire? Is it something valuable? Is it something lasting? Oh, why do we desire it? (1:183)

We are not angels but we have a body. To desire to be angels while we are on earth—and as much on earth as I was—is foolishness. (1:195)

True poverty of spirit . . . means being at rest in labors and dryness and not seeking consolation or comfort in prayer . . . but seeking consolation in trials for love of Him who always lived in the midst of them. (1:196–97)

How rich they will find that they are, they who have left all riches for Christ! . . . How wise they will be, they who rejoiced to be considered mad because that is what Wisdom Himself was called! (1:233)

Not all those of us who think we are detached, are in fact; it is necessary not to grow careless in this matter. (1:273)

It seemed to me I possessed all the world's riches in resolving to live by the love of God. (1:305)

The saying fits well here that the lost go after what is lost. And what greater perdition, greater blindness, greater misfortune than to cherish that which is nothing? (1:300)

I understood the great blessing there is in not paying attention to what doesn't bring us closer God. (1:355)

I think that even were I to possess many treasures, I wouldn't keep any special income or any money for myself alone, nor would this matter to me. I would only want to have what's necessary. . . . Although I don't desire any money for myself, I should like to have it so as to give it away. (1:374–75)

All that which ends with life is but a breath of wind. (1:453)

I want to live and die in striving and hoping for eternal life more than for the possession of all creatures and all their goods; for these will come to an end. (1:463)

Now since this is true, who will be able to say of himself that he is virtuous or rich? For at the very moment when there is need of virtue one finds oneself poor. (2:31)

God wants some to have an income, and in their case it's all right for them to worry about their income since that goes with their vocation. (2:43)

Worry about the financial resources of others, it seems to me, would amount to thinking about what others are enjoying. . . . Leave this worrying to the One who can move all, for He is the Lord of money and of those who earn money. (2:43–44)

Poverty of spirit is a good that includes within itself all the good things of the world. . . . Poverty of spirit embraces many of the virtues. In it lies great dominion. (2:45)

What do kings and lords matter to me if I don't want their riches, or don't care to please them if in order to do so I would have to displease God in even the smallest thing? (2:45)

Always remember that everything will come tumbling down on the day of judgment. Who knows whether this will come soon? (2:47)

A great aid to going against your will is to bear in mind continually how all is vanity and how quickly everything comes to an end. This helps to remove our attachment to trivia and center it on what will never end. (2:76)

All life is short, and the life of some extremely short. And how do we know if ours won't be so short that at the very hour or moment we determine to serve God completely it will come to an end? (2:82)

I consider it impossible for us to pay so much attention to worldly things if we take the care to remember we have a Guest such as this within us, for we then see how lowly these things are next to what we possess within ourselves. (2:144)

Yet the soul easily discerns that it is far different from earthly satisfactions and that ruling the world with all its delights wouldn't be enough to make the soul feel that delight within itself. (2:157)

What treasure do we have that could buy Your Son? The sale of Him, we already know, was for thirty pieces of silver. But to buy Him, no price is sufficient. (2:168)

To grow weary is quite foolish; for even though one does what's in one's power, what can those of us repay who, as I say, don't have anything save what we have received? All we can do is know ourselves and what we are capable of, which is to give our will, and give it completely. (2:164-65)

His Majesty gave strength and patience in such a way that even now I am amazed at how I was able to suffer, and I would not exchange those trials for all the world's treasures. (2:251)

Souls are still absorbed in the world and engulfed in their pleasures and vanities, with their honors and pre-tenses. . . . These souls are easily conquered, even though they may go about with desires not to offend God and though they do perform good works. (2:293)

Seek out someone who is very free from illusion about the things of the world. For in order to know ourselves, it helps a great deal to speak with someone who already knows the world for what it is. (2:314)

What we must do is beg like the needy poor before a rich and great emperor, and then lower our eyes and wait with humility. (2:329)

Our great God wants us to know our own misery and that He is king; and this is very important for what lies ahead. (2:365)

It is clearly revealed that He is the Lord of heaven and earth. This is not true of earthly kings. (2:412)

[The perfect] find all the happiness that could be wanted in this life, for in desiring nothing they possess all. (3:119)

I felt freedom in having so little esteem for temporal goods, for the lack of these goods brings an increase of interior good. Certainly, such a lack carries in its wake another kind of fullness and tranquility. (3:174–75)

Believe me, daughters, the means by which you think you are accumulating are those by which you will be losing. (3:246)

It seems to me comparable to taking many fish from the river with a net; they cannot live until they are in the water again. So it is with souls accustomed to living in the running streams of their Spouse. When taken out of them and caught up in the net of worldly things, they do not truly live until they find themselves back in those waters. (3:305–6)

THE FOURTH JOYFUL MYSTERY

THE PRESENTATION IN THE TEMPLE

Obedience

If you love me, you will keep my commandments.
—John 14:15

Let Your will be done in me in every way, and may it not please Your Majesty that something as precious as Your love be given to anyone who serves You only for the sake of consolations. (1:43–44)

We shouldn't care at all about not having devotion—as I have said—but we ought to thank the Lord who allows us to be desirous of pleasing Him, even though our works may be weak. This method of keeping Christ present with us is beneficial in all stages and is a very safe means of advancing. (1:120)

Everything other than pleasing God is nothing. (1:186)

No matter how much I did, I strove that it be done in such a way that it would not displease the One who I clearly saw was witnessing it. (1:237)

Nor does God ever fail anyone who serves Him. (1:303–4)

The Lord helps those who are resolved to render Him service and glory. (1:424)

There is only one all-powerful God and all three persons are one Majesty. Could one love the Father without loving the Son and the Holy Spirit? No, but anyone who pleases one of these three divine Persons, pleases all three, and the same goes for anyone who might offend one. (1:401)

Once while I was desiring to render some service to Our Lord, I was thinking about how little I was able to do for Him and I said to myself: "Why, Lord, do You desire my works?" He answered: "In order to see your will, daughter." (1:412)

May the Lord have a hand in all that I do so that it may conform to His holy will; these are my desires always, even though my works are as faulty as I am. (2:39)

Believe, Sisters, that if you serve His Majesty as you ought, you will not find better relatives than those He sends you. (2:74)

❧

May the Lord, because of who He is, give us light to follow His will in everything, and there will be nothing to fear. (2:106)

Those in the world will be doing enough if they truly have the determination to do His will. You, daughters, will express this determination by both saying and doing, by both words and deeds. (2:163)

Unless we give our wills entirely to the Lord so that in everything pertaining to us He might do what conforms with His will, we will never be allowed to drink from this fount. Drinking from it is perfect contemplation. (2:163)

Therefore, if we please the Lord, those in hell will be kept bound; they will not do anything that may be harmful to us however much they might draw us into temptation and set secret snares for us. (2:197)

Have the right intention, a resolute will, as I have said, not to offend God. Don't let your soul withdraw into a corner, for instead of obtaining sanctity you will obtain many imperfections. (2:200)

Such a person must not live for his own will but for the will of his King. (2:202)

But knowing that the strength given by obedience usually lessens the difficulty of things that seem impossible, I resolved to carry out the task very willingly, even though my human nature seems greatly distressed. (2:281)

[Love] doesn't consist in great delight but in desiring with strong determination to please God in everything, in striving, insofar as possible, not to offend Him, and in asking Him for the advancement of the honor and glory of His Son. (2:272)

Don't think that in what concerns perfection there is some mystery or things unknown or still to be understood, for in perfect conformity to God's will lies all our good. (2:301)

Shouldn't we consider ourselves lucky to be able to repay something of what we owe Him for His service toward us? . . . The fact is that He did nothing else but serve us all the time He lived in this world. (2:308)

Doing our own will is usually what harms us. (2:314)

We belong to Him, daughters. Let Him do whatever He likes with us, bring us wherever He pleases. (2:326)

Once the great King . . . sees their good will, He desires in His wonderful mercy to bring them back to Him. Like a good shepherd, with a whistle so gentle that even they themselves almost fail to hear it, He makes them recognize His voice. (2:328)

There is every reason to be conformed to the will of God. (2:393)

Our security lies in obedience and refusal to deviate from God's law. (2:348–49)

This union with God's will is the union I have desired all my life; it is the union I ask the Lord for always and the one that is clearest and safest. (2:350)

Since we know the path by which we must please God, which is that of the commandments and counsels, we should follow it very diligently, and think of His life and death and of the many things we owe Him; let the rest come when the Lord desires. (2:401)

I have seen through experience the great good that comes to a soul when it does not turn aside from obedience. It is through this practice that I think one advances in virtue and gains humility. (3:95)

Well, come now, my daughters, don't be sad when obedience draws you to involvement in exterior matters. Know that if it is in the kitchen, the Lord walks among the pots and pans helping you both interiorly and exteriorly. (3:119–20)

The Lord esteems this surrender very much, and rightly so, because it means making Him Lord over the free will He has given us. (3:121)

He is pleased more by obedience than by sacrifice. Well, if this is true and if I merit more, why am I disturbed? (3:133)

What His Majesty desires cannot be set aside. (3:214)

THE FIFTH JOYFUL MYSTERY

THE FINDING OF THE CHILD JESUS IN THE TEMPLE

Piety

You . . . must be perfect, as your heavenly Father is perfect.
—Matthew 5:48

With Your favor and through Your mercy I can say what St. Paul said, although not with such perfection, that I no longer live but that You, my Creator, live in me. (1:81)

Whoever has not begun the practice of prayer, I beg for the love of the Lord not to go without so great a good. There is nothing here to fear but only something to desire. Even if there be no great progress, or much effort in reaching such perfection . . . at least a person will come to understand the road leading to heaven. (1:96)

Hardly ever did a sermon seem so bad to me that I didn't listen to it eagerly, even though according to others who heard it the preaching was not good. . . . After I had begun the practice of prayer, speaking of God or hearing others speak of Him hardly ever tired me. (1:100)

If beginners with the assistance of God struggle to reach the summit of perfection, I believe they will never go to heaven alone; they will always lead many people along after them. Like good captains they will give whoever marches in their company to God. (1:112)

Once you are placed in so high a degree as to desire to commune in solitude with God and abandon the pastimes of the world, the most has been done. (1:116)

Experience is a great help in all, for it teaches what is suitable for us; and God can be served in everything. (1:118)

For if [the saints] had never determined to desire and seek this state little by little in practice they would never have mounted so high. His Majesty wants this determination, and He is a friend of courageous souls if they walk in humility and without trusting in self. (1:123–24)

Just as there are many mansions in heaven, there are many paths. (1:129)

It was a great delight for me to consider my soul as a garden and reflect that the Lord was taking His walk in it. I begged Him to increase the fragrance of the little flowers of virtue that were beginning to bloom, so it seemed, and that they might give Him glory and He might sustain them. (1:137)

Blessed is the soul the Lord brings to the understanding of truth! Oh, how fit a state this is for kings! (1:185)

❧

The more that love and humility grow, the greater the fragrance these flowers of virtues give off, both for oneself and for others. (1:188)

When one is in the midst of business matters, and in times of persecutions and trials, when one can't maintain so much quietude, and in times of dryness, Christ is a very good friend. . . . He is company for us. Once we have the habit, it is very easy to find Him present at our side. (1:196)

Desires are restless and the soul never succeeds in being satisfied. This is the experience of those to whom God gives the great impulses of love. . . . These impulses are like some little springs I've seen flowing; they never cease to move the sand upward. (1:262)

Little by little one makes progress in deeds. And His Majesty gives value to little things like these that are done for Him, and He gives the help for doing greater things.
(1:275)

They who really love You, my Good, walk safely on a broad and royal road. They are far from the precipice. Hardly have they begun to stumble when You, Lord, give them Your hand. (1:308)

I cannot understand what it is that makes people afraid of setting out on the road of perfection. . . . True security lies in striving to make progress on the road of God. (1:308–9)

One person in half a year can gain more than another can in twenty years because, as I say, the Lord gives to whomever He wants and also to whoever is better disposed. (1:346)

Teach by works more than by words. (1:435)

Now is the time to take what this compassionate Lord and God of ours gives us. Since He desires our friendship, who will deny it to one who did not refuse to shed all His blood and lose His life for us? Behold that what He asks for is nothing, since giving it is for our own benefit. (1:458)

One who is perfect will do much more than many who are not. (2:49)

Clearly, we must work hard, and it helps a great deal to have lofty thoughts so that we will exert ourselves and make our deeds comply with our thoughts. (2:53)

I want to say a little about this love. . . . For when virtue is placed before our eyes, the one who desires it grows fond of it and seeks to gain it. (2:62)

The imitation of the virtue in which one sees another excel has a great tendency to spread. This is good advice; don't forget it. (2:69)

It is true that these virtues have the characteristic of so hiding themselves from the person who possesses them that he never sees them or manages to believe that he has them.... But he esteems them so highly that he always goes about striving to obtain them, and he gradually perfects them within himself. (2:77)

In fact, there is a holy simplicity that knows little about the affairs and style of the world but a lot about dealing with God. (2:89)

We must all try to be preachers through our deeds. (2:92)

It is a great good to think that if we try we can become saints with God's help. And have no fear that He will fail if we don't fail. Since we have not come here for any other thing, let us put our hands to the task. (2:98)

However great the abundance of this water He gives, there cannot be too much in anything of His. If He gives a great deal, He gives the soul, as I said, the capacity to drink much; like a glassmaker who makes the vessel a size he sees is necessary in order to hold what he intends to pour into it. (2:111)

In the measure you desire Him, you will find Him. He so esteems our turning to look at Him that no diligence will be lacking on His part. (2:134)

If you grow accustomed to having Him present at your side, and He sees that you do so with love and that you go about striving to please Him, you will not be able—as they say—to get away from Him; He will never fail you; He will help you in all your trials; you will find Him everywhere. (2:133)

Since He doesn't force our will, He takes what we give Him; but He doesn't give Himself completely until we give ourselves completely. (2:145)

He suffers and will suffer everything in order to find even one soul that will receive Him and lovingly keep Him within. (2:175)

There must be a war in this life. In the face of so many enemies it's not possible for us to sit with our hands folded; there must always be this care about how we are proceeding interiorly and exteriorly. (2:223)

Oh, how happy will be the lot of one who obtains this favor since it is a union with the will of God.... It is a union not based on words or desires alone, but a union proved by deeds. (2:236)

Let us understand, my daughters, that true perfection consists in love of God and neighbor; the more perfectly we keep these two commandments the more perfect we will be. (2:295–96)

Those souls that are good and humble will praise Him much more. (2:314)

The whole aim of any person who is beginning prayer—and don't forget this, because it's very important—should be that he work and prepare himself with determination and every possible effort to bring his will into conformity with God's will. . . . The greatest perfection attainable along the spiritual path lies in this conformity. (2:301)

Love is never idle, and a failure to grow would be a very bad sign. (2:357–58)

Oh, how desirable is this union with God's will! Happy the soul that has reached it. Such a soul will live tranquilly in this life, and in the next as well. Nothing in earthly events afflicts it. (2:349)

I would want you to praise Him often, Sisters, for the one who begins, awakens the others. In what better way can you, when together, use your tongues than in the praises of God since we have so many reasons for praising Him? (2:396)

I repeat, it is necessary that your foundation consist of more than prayer and contemplation. If you do not strive for the virtues and practice them, you will always be dwarfs. . . . Whoever does not increase decreases. (2:447)

The person who knows God better does God's work more easily. (3:108)

In this matter God greatly favors me, for when there was question of work to be done I enjoyed being the first. (3:194)

Oh, my daughters, everything that helps us advance is important. (3:279)

> Keep ready your oil jar
> Of merit and deeds,
> Ample to keep
> Your lamp aflame
> Lest outside you be kept
> When He comes.
> *Do not be careless.* (3:402)

THE
SORROWFUL
MYSTERIES

THE FIRST SORROWFUL MYSTERY

THE AGONY OF JESUS IN THE GARDEN

Sorrow for Sin

The cares of the world, and the delight in riches, and the desire for other things, enter in and choke the word, and it proves unfruitful.—Mark 4:19

Many times the feeling of my great faults is tempered by the happiness experienced in the thought that the multitude of Your mercies may be known. (1:65)

I found great consolation in sinners whom, after having been sinners, the Lord brought back to Himself. It seemed to me I could find help in them and that since the Lord had pardoned them He could also pardon me. (1:103)

Oh, what a good friend You make, my Lord! How you proceed by favoring and enduring.... You take into account, my Lord, the times when they love You, and in one instant of repentance You forget their offenses. (1:97)

The scene of His prayer in the garden, especially, was a comfort to me; I strove to be His companion there. If I could, I thought of the sweat and agony He had undergone in that place.... I remained with Him as long as my thoughts allowed me to. (1:101)

Where, my Lord, did I think I could find a remedy save in You? What folly; to flee from the light so as to be always stumbling! (1:169)

O my Jesus! What a sight it is when You through Your mercy return to offer Your hand and raise up a soul that has fallen in sin.... How such a soul knows the multitude of Your grandeurs and mercies and its own misery!
(1:166–67)

Once I understood a thing to be a mortal sin, I then avoided it. (1:73)

I believe matters become worse if one abandons prayer and doesn't amend one's evil ways. But if people don't abandon it, they may believe that prayer will bring them to the harbor of light. (1:166)

For the love of God we should avoid the occasions; the Lord will help us, as He did me. May it please His Majesty not to let me out of His hand lest I fall again, for I have already seen where I would end up. (1:279)

One fall is not sufficient for a person to be lost, nor are many, if they love You and not the things of the world. They journey in the valley of humility. (1:308)

❦

I saw that He was a man, even though He was God; that He wasn't surprised by human weaknesses; that He understands our miserable make-up, subject to many falls on account of the first sin which He came to repair. I can speak with Him as with a friend, even though He is Lord. (1:325)

I saw clearly how much the Lord did on His part, from the time I was a little child, to bring me to Himself. . . . The excessive love God has in pardoning us for all [our] failure when we want to return to Him was made clearly manifest to me. (1:391–92)

You are mighty, great God! Now it can be known whether my soul understands itself in being aware of the time it has lost and of how in a moment You, Lord, can win this time back again. . . . They usually say lost time cannot be recovered. May You be blessed, my God!
(1:446–47)

My ransom cost You a great deal. (1:449)

Oh, what a pity! Oh, what great blindness, that we seek rest where it is impossible to find it! (1:450)

Realize that all the devil's joys and promises are false and traitorous.... What can we expect from him who was against You? (1:455)

O mortals, return, return to yourselves! Behold your King, for now you will find Him meek.... Turn your fury and your strength against the one who makes war on you and wants to take away your birthright. (1:455)

Let us try hard, let us trust hard, for you know that His Majesty says that if we are sorry for having offended Him our faults and evils will not be remembered. Oh, compassion so measureless! (1:458)

Hasn't He already paid far more than enough for the sin of Adam? Whenever we sin again must this loving Lamb pay? ... Do not look at our sins but behold that Your most blessed Son redeemed us. (2:51)

We must never tire of condemning anything that leads to hell, for the slightest evil of hell cannot be exaggerated. (2:66)

If you are experiencing trials or are sad, behold Him on the way to the garden: what great affliction He bore in His soul; for having become suffering itself.... Or behold Him bound to the column, filled with pain, with all His flesh torn in pieces for the great love He bears you. (2:134)

He must bear with us no matter how serious the offenses. If we return to Him like the prodigal son, He has to pardon us. He has to console us in our trials. He has to sustain us in the way a father like this must. (2:138)

All the harm comes from not truly understanding that He is near, but in imagining Him as far away. (2:147)

With regard to these enemies, daughters, let us ask and often beg the Lord in the Our Father to free us and not let us walk into temptation, so they will not draw us into error or hide the light and truth from us. (2:185)

Now be also on your guard, daughters, against some types of humility given by the devil in which great disquiet is felt about the gravity of our sins. This disturbance can afflict in many ways even to the point of making one give up receiving Communion and practicing private prayer. These things are given up because the devil makes one feel unworthy. (2:189)

When you find yourselves in this condition, stop thinking about your misery, insofar as possible, and turn your thoughts to the mercy of God, to how He loves us and suffered for us. (2:190)

Be careful and attentive—this is very important—until you see that you are strongly determined not to offend the Lord, that you would lose a thousand lives rather than commit a mortal sin, and that you are most careful not to commit venial sins—that is, advertently. (2:197)

Consider, Sisters, for the love of God, if you want to gain this fear of the Lord, that it is very helpful to understand the seriousness of an offense against God and to reflect on this frequently in your thoughts; for it is worth our life and much more to have this virtue rooted in our souls. (2:197–98)

I was given understanding of what it is for a soul to be in mortal sin. It amounts to clouding this mirror with mist and leaving it black; and thus this Lord cannot be revealed or seen even though He is always present giving us being. (2:269)

To fall into mortal sin, there's no darker darkness nor anything more obscure and black. . . . Although the very sun that gave the soul so much brilliance and beauty is still in the center, the soul is as though it were not there to share in these things. (2:288)

In sum, since the tree is planted where the devil is, what fruit can it bear? (2:289)

Avoid the occasions of sin. This failure to avoid these occasions is quite dangerous. (2:297)

These joys the devil gives it are filled with trials, cares, and contradictions. . . . Neither security nor peace will be found. (2:299)

What hope can we have of finding rest outside of ourselves if we cannot be at rest within. . . . Well, believe me, if we don't obtain and have peace in our own house we'll not find it outside. Let this war be ended. (2:302)

There will always be failures as long as we live in this mortal body. (2:398)

His Majesty knows how to draw good from evil, and the road along which the devil wanted to make you go astray will be to your greater gain. (2:415)

Well, if the passions go unmortified, and each passion seeks to get what it wants, what would happen if no one resisted them? (3:135)

This self-love of ours is such that it's a wonder if we ever blame ourselves, nor do we know ourselves. (3:353)

Ah, how bitter a life
When the Lord is not enjoyed! (3:376)

The Second Sorrowful Mystery

The Scourging at the Pillar

Purity

Clean the inside of the cup and dish first so that the outside may become clean as well. — Matthew 23:26

What a danger it is at an age when one should begin to cultivate the virtues to associate with people who do not know the vanity of the world but rather are just getting ready to throw themselves into it. (1:57)

My soul began to return to the good habits of early childhood, and I saw the great favor God accords to anyone placed with good companions. (1:60)

This good company began to help me get rid of the habits that the bad company had caused and to turn my mind to the desire for eternal things. (1:61)

Women are obligated to modesty more than men. (1:73)

He wants it [the soul] alone and clean and desirous of receiving His graces. If we place many stumbling blocks in His path and don't do a thing to remove them, how will He be able to come to us? And we desire God to grant us great favors! (1:99)

Beginners must realize that in order to give delight to the Lord they are starting to cultivate a garden on very barren soil, full of abominable weeds. His Majesty pulls up the weeds and plants good seed. (1:113)

Be very much on guard against sinning. . . . What I advise strongly is not to abandon prayer, for in prayer people will understand what they are doing and win repentance from the Lord and fortitude to lift themselves up. And you must believe that if you give up prayer, you are, in my opinion, courting danger. (1:140)

I only think that the soul comes out of the crucible like gold, more refined and purified, so as to see the Lord within itself. So afterward these trials that seemed unbearable become small. (1:260)

I was amazed afterward how this fire, when one is united to it, seems to consume the old man with his faults and lukewarmness and misery. Like the phoenix . . . which after it is burned rises again from the same ashes, so afterward the soul becomes another, with different desires and great fortitude. It doesn't seem to be what it was before, but begins to walk on the Lord's path with new purity. (1:352)

The soul is like water in a glass: the water looks very clear if the sun doesn't shine on it; but when the sun shines on it, it seems to be full of dust particles. (1:184)

❦

True security is the testimony of a good conscience. (1:397)

I understood that [union with God] consists in the spirit being pure and raised above all earthly things so that there is nothing in the soul that wants to turn aside from God's will. (1:398)

I've seen the vision of the Blessed Trinity and how it dwells in a soul in the state of grace. (1:400)

You already know that the cornerstone must be a good conscience and that with all your strength you must strive to free yourselves even from venial sins and seek what is the most perfect. (2:59)

Everything done with a pure intention is perfect love. (2:69)

Get rid of this pestilence; cut off the branches as best you can, and if this is not enough pull up the roots. (2:71)

For although interiorly it takes time to become totally detached and mortified, exteriorly it must be done immediately. (2:88)

Well, let us imagine that within us is an extremely rich palace.... There is no edifice as beautiful as is a soul pure and full of virtues. The greater the virtues the more resplendent the jewels. (2:143)

It involves a gradual increase of self-control and an end to vain wandering from the right path; it means conquering, which is a making use of one's senses for the sake of the inner life. (2:148)

It is almost impossible for us to understand the sublime dignity and beauty of the soul. (2:284)

If I had understood as I do now that in this little palace of my soul dwelt so great a King, I would not have left Him alone so often. (2:144)

In what better way could we be occupied than to prepare rooms within our souls for our Spouse? ... Happy will be the soul that makes this request and whose lamp will not be out when the Lord comes. (2:224)

It's true that we cannot live without faults, but at least there should be some change so that they don't take root. If they take root, they will be harder to eradicate and even many others could arise from them. (2:230)

And when the active works rise from this interior root, they become lovely and very fragrant flowers. For they proceed from this tree of God's love and are done for

Him alone, without any self-interest. The fragrance from these flowers spreads to the benefit of many. (2:257)

Because we have heard and because faith tells us so, we know we have souls. But we seldom consider the precious things that can be found in this soul, or who dwells within it, or its high value. Consequently, little effort is made to preserve its beauty. (2:284)

Just as all the streams that flow from a crystal-clear fount are also clear, the works of a soul in grace, because they proceed from this fount of life, in which the soul is planted like a tree, are most pleasing in the eyes of both God and man. (2:288–89)

If we are always fixed on our earthly misery, the stream will never flow free from the mud of fears, faintheartedness, and cowardice. (2:292)

It should be kept in mind here that the fount, the shining sun that is in the center of the soul, does not lose its beauty and splendor; it is always present in the soul, and nothing can take away its loveliness. But if a black cloth is placed over a crystal that is in the sun, obviously the sun's brilliance will have no effect on the crystal. (2:289)

I am certain the Lord never fails to give a person like this security of conscience, which is no small blessing. (2:304)

For little things happen . . . in which you can very well test and know whether or not you are the rulers of your passions. (2:311)

The truth is that the treasure lies within our very selves. (2:336)

God espouses souls spiritually. Blessed be His mercy that wants so much to be humbled! . . . It is all a matter of love united with love, and the actions of love are most pure and so extremely delicate and gentle that there is no way of explaining them. (2:354)

The devil needs nothing more than to see a little door open before playing a thousand tricks on us. (2:416)

Just as in heaven so in the soul His Majesty must have a room where He dwells alone. Let us call it another heaven. (2:428)

He and the Father and the Holy Spirit will come to dwell with the soul that loves Him and keeps His commandments. . . . If the soul does not fail God, He will never fail, in my opinion, to make His presence clearly known to it. (2:430–31)

If we proceed with a pure conscience and obediently, the Lord will never permit the devil to have enough

influence to deceive harmfully our souls; on the contrary, the devil himself is the one who is left deceived.
(3:113–14)

Consider that through very little things the door is opened to very big things, and that without your realizing it the world will start entering your lives. (3:245)

When one is rooted in virtue, the occasions of sin are of little consequence. (3:285)

The Third Sorrowful Mystery

The Crowning with Thorns

Courage

Courage! It is I! Do not be afraid.
—Matthew 14:27

I don't understand these fears, "The devil! The devil!", when we can say "God! God!", and make the devil tremble. (1:29)

I would never counsel anyone—if there were someone to whom I should have to give counsel—to fail out of fear to put a good inspiration into practice when it repeatedly arises. For if one proceeds with detachment for God alone, there is no reason to fear that the effort will turn out bad; for God has the power to accomplish all. (1:65)

His Majesty wants this determination, and He is a friend of courageous souls if they walk in humility and without trusting in self. (1:124)

By considering the love He bore me, I regained my courage, for I never lost confidence in His mercy. (1:103)

God does not deny Himself to anyone who perseveres. Little by little He will measure out the courage sufficient to attain this victory. I say "courage" because there are so many things the devil puts in the minds of beginners to prevent them in fact from starting out on this path. (1:112)

Since we have an all-powerful King and so great a Lord that He can do all and that He brings all under His subjection, there is nothing to fear, if one walks, as I have said, in truth in the presence of His Majesty and with a pure conscience. (1:223–24)

The Lord Himself pointed out this way of perfection saying: *take up your cross and follow me*. He is our model; whoever follows His counsels solely for the sake of pleasing Him has nothing to fear. (1:146)

Prayer is the source of heroic promises, of resolutions, and of ardent desires; it is the beginning of contempt for the world because of a clear perception of the world's vanity. (1:164)

I can do all things, providing You do not leave me. Were You to leave, for however short a time, I would return to where I was. (1:187)

I consider this courage the Lord gave me ... one of the great favors He granted me. For that a soul should be intimidated by or fearful of anything other than offending God is a serious disadvantage. (1:223)

❧

The devil does a great deal to incapacitate us when he sees a little fear. (1:125)

If this Lord is all powerful, as I see that He is and I know that He is, ... what evil can they do to me since I am a servant of this Lord and King? Why shouldn't I have the fortitude to engage in combat with all of hell? (1:222)

The true servant of God might pay no attention to the scarecrows the devils set up in order to cause fear. We should know that each time we pay no attention to them they are weakened, and the soul gains much more mastery. Some great benefit always remains. (1:267)

It is very necessary for this weak nature of ours to have great confidence and not grow faint-hearted or start thinking that even if we make efforts we shall still fail to gain the victory. (1:272)

God has given me great courage; and the greater these trials were the greater was the courage. (1:383)

They must have a great and very resolute determination to persevere until reaching the end, come what may, happen what may, whatever work is involved, whatever criticism arises, whether they arrive or whether they die on the road, or even if they don't have courage for the trials that are met, or if the whole world collapses. (2:34)

If you do what lies in your power, the Lord will make you so strong that you will astonish men. And how easy this is for His Majesty since He made us from nothing. (2:70)

Whoever has them [sovereign virtues] can easily go out and fight with all hell together and against the whole world and all its occasions of sin. Such a person has no fear of anyone, for his is the kingdom of heaven. (2:77)

I truly believe that the Lord highly favors the one who has real determination. (2:88)

He is the true friend, and through this friendship I find in myself a dominion by which it seems to me I could resist, providing God doesn't fail me, anyone who might be against me. (1:382)

What would it matter, when you are in the arms of God, if the whole world blamed you! He has the power to free you from everything, for once He commanded that the world be made, it was made; His will is the deed. (2:97)

The presumption I would like to see present in this house, for it always makes humility grow, is to have a holy daring; for God helps the strong and He shows no partiality. (2:98)

It is good for the Lord to know we are doing our best. We must be like soldiers who even though they may not have served a great deal must always be ready for any duty the captain commands them to undertake. . . . And how much better the pay our King gives than the pay of earthly kings. (2:103)

Oh, the greatness of God, for sometimes one or two men alone can do more when they speak the truth than many together! Little by little, souls discover again the way; God gives them courage. (2:120)

Thus, since there are one or two who fearlessly do what is best, the Lord at once begins to win back gradually the ground that was lost. (2:120-21)

The devil [is] extremely afraid of determined souls, for he has experienced the great harm they do him. And all the harm he plans to do them turns out to their benefit and to that of others as well; and he comes out with a loss. (2:126-27)

I say there are so many reasons why it is extremely important to begin with great determination. . . . There is no reason to failing to give with complete determination.
(2:125)

When we are more determined we are less confident of ourselves, for confidence must be placed in God. When we understand this that I said about ourselves, there will be no need to go about so tense and constrained; the Lord will protect us. (2:198)

Be certain that the Lord will never fail His lovers, when they take a risk for Him alone. (2:239)

Thus, my daughters, strive to think rightly about God, for He doesn't look at trifles as much as you think, and don't lose your courage or allow your soul to be constrained, for many blessings could be lost. (2:200)

I repeat and ask that you always have courageous thoughts. As a result of them the Lord will give you grace for courageous deeds. Believe that these brave thoughts are important. (2:230)

Oh, strong love of God! And how true it is that nothing seems impossible to the one who loves! Oh, happy the soul that has obtained this peace from its God, for it is master over all the trials and dangers of the world, fears no one provided it serves so good a Spouse and Lord. (2:238)

I tell you there is need for more courage than you think. (2:274)

Let the soul always heed the warning not to be conquered.... Be determined to fight with all the devils and realize that there are no better weapons than those of the cross. (2:300)

When we see some things done by others that seem so impossible for us and the ease with which they are done, we become very encouraged. And it seems that through the flight of these others we also will make bold to fly, as do the bird's fledglings when they are taught; for even they do not begin to soar immediately, little by little they imitate the parent. (2:314)

God is so faithful that He will not allow the devil much leeway with a soul that doesn't aim for anything else than to please His Majesty.... If He sometimes permits the devil to tempt the soul, He will so ordain that the evil one will be defeated. (2:409)

When You, Lord, want to give courage, how little do all contradictions matter! Rather, it seems I am encouraged by them, thinking that since the devil is beginning to be disturbed the Lord will be served. (3:107)

How does one acquire this love? By being determined to work and to suffer, and to do so when the occasion arises. It is indeed true that by thinking of what we owe the Lord, of who He is, and what we are, a soul's determination grows, and that this thinking is very meritorious and appropriate. (3:117)

How could it be known whether a man were valiant if he were not seen in battle? St. Peter thought he was very courageous; see how he acted when the occasion presented itself. (3:123)

His Majesty defends those who are without fault. (3:236)

To have life is to live in such a way that there is no fear of death or of any of life's happenings, to have an habitual happiness.... To what can the interior and exterior peace that you always enjoy be compared? It is in your power to live and to die with this peace. (3:245)

If you have confidence in Him and have courageous spirits—for His Majesty is very fond of these—you need not fear that He will fail you in anything. (3:245)

I was surprised and reflected on how very important it is not to consider our weak state of health or any opposition that occurs when we understand that something serves the Lord since God is powerful enough to make the weak strong and the sick healthy. (3:257)

Great is the power of holiness and virtue. (3:267)

> Let nothing trouble you,
> Let nothing scare you,
> All is fleeting,
> God alone is unchanging. (3:386)

Since love
Has given us God
No reason is there to fear. . . . (3:389)

Opponents we conquer
In following this way.
At last we will rest in
The Maker of Heaven and Earth. (3:397)

The Fourth Sorrowful Mystery

The Carrying of the Cross

Patience

As for [the seeds] in the good soil, they are those who, hearing the word, hold it fast in an honest and good heart, and bring forth fruit with patience.—Luke 8:15

Oh, what a good friend You make, my Lord! How You proceed by favoring and enduring. You wait for others to adapt to Your nature, and in the meanwhile You put up with theirs! (1:43)

He bestows a strong desire to advance in prayer and not abandon it no matter what trial may come upon one. The soul offers itself up in all things. (1:146)

Whoever lives in the presence of so good a friend and excellent a leader, who went ahead of us to be the first to suffer, can endure all things. The Lord helps us, strengthens us, and never fails. (1:194)

What more do we desire than to have such a good friend at our side, who will not abandon us in our labors and tribulations, as friends in the world do? Blessed are they who truly love Him and always keep Him at their side! Let us consider the glorious St. Paul: it doesn't seem that any other name fell from his lips than that of Jesus. (1:194)

He showed me His wounds in order to encourage me when I was suffering tribulation. (1:247)

I complained to Him for consenting that I should suffer so many torments. But this suffering was well repaid, for almost always the favors afterward came in great abundance. I only think that the soul comes out of the crucible like gold, more refined and purified, so as to see the Lord within itself. (1:260)

If someone is not perfect, I say that more courage is necessary to follow the path to perfection than to suffer a quick martyrdom. For perfection is not attained quickly, unless the Lord wants to grant someone this favor by a special privilege. (1:271)

Watch with care, for everything passes quickly. . . . Behold the more you struggle the more you show the love you have for your God and the more you will rejoice in your Beloved with a joy and delight that cannot end. (1:459)

We have other faults, which makes it right for us to practice patience. (2:322)

Everything seems to be a heavy burden, and rightly so, because it involves a war against ourselves. But once we begin to work, God does so much in the soul and grants it so many favors that all that one can do in this life seems little. (2:81)

❦

Sometimes the Lord comes very late and pays just as well, and all at once, what He was giving to others in the course of many years. (2:99)

Be patient and leave it in the hands of God. . . . In every event the best we can do is leave ourselves in the hands of God. (2:112)

Do not fear that you will die of thirst on this road. Never is the lack of consoling water such that it cannot be endured. (2:114)

If he [the devil] knows that someone is changeable and unstable in being good and not strongly determined to persevere, he will keep after him day and night; he will cause fears and never-ending obstacles. I know this very well through experience. . . . No one knows how important determination is. (2:127)

He should not grow anxious, which makes things worse. (2:130)

Behold Him burdened with the cross, for they didn't even let Him take a breath. He will look at you with those eyes so beautiful and compassionate, filled with tears; He will forget His sorrows so as to console you in yours, merely because you yourselves go to Him to be consoled, and you turn your head to look at Him. (2:134–35)

He knows what each one can suffer. He does not delay in doing His will in anyone He sees has strength. (2:161–62)

When you suffer often, praise God that He is beginning to teach you this virtue of patience and strive to endure. . . . He gives it to you, and you do not possess it save as though on deposit. (2:188)

When you feel this [timidity], have recourse to faith and humility, and don't fail to go on fighting with faith, for God can do all. (2:238)

Oh, great dignity, worthy of awakening us that we might try diligently to please this Lord and King of ours! . . . Indeed, how great is the mercy of God. Where would we find a friend so patient? (2:230)

Peacefully and quietly the soul will conquer the world. (2:240)

His Majesty knows well how to wait many days and years, especially when He sees perseverance and good desires. This perseverance is most necessary here. One always gains much through perseverance. (2:298)

Provided that we don't give up, the Lord will guide everything for our benefit. (2:303)

[The soul's] faith is more alive; it knows that if it suffers trials for God, His Majesty will give it the grace to suffer them with patience. (2:332)

In sum, there is no remedy in this tempest but to wait for the mercy of God. For at an unexpected time, with one word alone or a chance happening, He so quickly calms the storm that it seems there had never been as much as a cloud in that soul. (2:364)

However long it lasts, it lasts but a moment in comparison with eternity. (2:412)

For the storms, like a wave, pass quickly. And the fair weather returns. (2:443)

I understand clearly that what I did for my part was little, but God wants no more than our determination so that He may do everything Himself. (3:257)

We will finish our day's journey, for it goes by so quickly and all comes to an end. (3:264)

> If You want me to rest,
> I desire it for love;
> If to labor,
> I will die working:
> . . . Calvary or Tabor give me,
> Desert or fruitful land;
> As Job in suffering
> Or John at Your breast;
> Barren or fruited vine,
> Whatever be Your will:
> *What do you want of me?* (3:378–79)

> Patience
> Everything obtains.
> Who possesses God
> Nothing wants.
> God alone suffices. (3:386)

The Fifth Sorrowful Mystery

The Crucifixion

Self-Denial

If any man would come after me, let him deny himself and take up his cross daily and follow me. —Luke 9:23

Even in sickness itself and these other occasions the prayer is genuine when it comes from a soul that loves to offer the sickness up and accept what is happening and be conformed to it. (1:88)

All bear their crosses even though these crosses be different. For all who follow Christ, if they don't want to get lost, must walk along this path that He trod. And blessed be the trials that even here in this life are so superabundantly repaid. (1:112)

There are many who begin, yet they never reach the end. I believe this is due mainly to a failure to embrace the cross from the beginning. (1:117)

If people wish to gain freedom of spirit and not be always troubled, let them begin by not being frightened by the cross, and they will see how the Lord also helps them carry it and they will gain satisfaction and profit from everything. (1:119)

We have such stingy hearts that it seems to us we're going to lose the earth if we desire to neglect the body a little for the sake of the spirit. . . . It makes me sad that we have so little confidence in God and so much self love that these concerns should disturb us. (1:125)

Embracing the cross, come what may, is an important thing. This Lord was deprived of every consolation; they left Him alone in His trials. Let us not abandon Him, for He will give us better support than our own efforts that we might ascend higher. (1:196)

I was anxious to know the manner and way in which I could do penance for so much evil and merit something in order to gain so much good. . . . My spirit was not at rest, yet the disquiet was not a disturbing but a delightful one. (1:279)

His Majesty also told me He was clearly aware of my trial, but that it couldn't be otherwise while I lived in this exile, that everything was for my greater good; and He consoled me very much. (1:433)

I look very differently upon what the Lord suffered, as something belonging to me—and it gives me great comfort. (1:412)

I have seen it clearly and recall how much the Lord will suffer for only one soul. (1:362)

❦

You say, My Lord, that You come to seek sinners.... Don't look at our blindness, my God, but at all the blood Your Son shed for us. Let your mercy shine upon evil that has so increased. (1:451)

I desire, Lord, to please You.... If it's necessary to live in order to render You some service, I don't refuse all the trials that can come to me on earth. (1:459)

If I ask You to free me from a trial, and the purpose of that trial is my mortification, what is it that I'm asking for, my God? (1:461)

Now, then, the first thing we must strive for is to rid ourselves of our love for our bodies, for some of us are by nature such lovers of comfort that there is no small amount of work in this area. (2:77)

The devil suggests that you indulge yourselves. (2:78)

It seems to me an imperfection, my Sisters, to be always complaining about light illnesses. If you can tolerate them, don't complain about them. (2:79)

A fault this body has is that the more comfort we try to give it the more needs it discovers. It's amazing how much comfort it wants.... The poor soul is deceived and doesn't grow. (2:80)

Remember how many sick people there are who are poor and have no one to complain to.... Learn how to suffer a little for love of God without having everyone know about it. (2:80)

Shouldn't we suffer just between ourselves and God some of the illnesses He gives us because of our sins? And even more so because by our complaining the sickness is not alleviated. (2:80)

If we do not determine once and for all to swallow death and the lack of health, we will never do anything. Strive not to fear them; abandon yourselves totally to God, come what may. So what if we die? If our body has so mocked us so often, shouldn't we mock it at least once? (2:81)

Little by little as we grow accustomed to this attitude we shall, with the Lord's help, remain lords of our bodies ... a very important means to enduring the battle of this life. (2:81)

Interior mortification makes everything else more meritorious and perfect, and afterward enables us to do the other things with greater ease and repose. (2:82)

This interior mortification is acquired, as I have said, by proceeding gradually, not giving in to our own will and appetites, even in little things, until the body is completely surrendered to the spirit. (2:82)

I repeat that the whole matter, or a great part of it, lies in losing concern about ourselves and our own satisfaction. The least that any of us who has truly begun to serve the Lord can offer Him is our own life. Since we have given the Lord our will, what do we fear? (2:82)

So, let us try hard to go against our own will in everything. For if you are careful, as I have said, you will gradually, without knowing how, find yourselves at the summit. (2:82)

If you wish to take revenge on the devil and free yourself more quickly from temptation, ... do some lowly task; or, if possible, do it on your own and go about studying how to double your willingness to do things that go contrary to your nature. The Lord will reveal these things to you. (2:84)

Now, then, to enjoy a part in His kingdom and want no part in His dishonors and trials is nonsense. (2:86)

And from very little things, as I have said at other times, one can gain the light so as to come out the victor in great things. (2:91)

In the beginning it is difficult; but I know that such freedom, self-denial, and detachment from ourselves can, with God's help, be attained. (2:93)

Mortification helps in everything. (2:112)

The flesh is very fond of comfort. . . . If we could understand we would realize that to seek one's peace in comforts is very dangerous. . . . The body grows fat and the soul weakens. (2:228)

What I am saying is that we must not find our rest in being lax, but must test ourselves sometimes. I know that this flesh is very deceptive and that we need to understand it. (2:229)

They begin to make progress and then falter on the road. . . . These souls are not exercised in mortification and in denying their own will, and so they never get over their fear. (2:235)

If trials are not suffered for God, they are worth nothing; if they are suffered for Him, His Majesty adapts them to our strength. Thus, if we are so afraid of them it is because we are fainthearted. (2:246)

To the little we do, which is nothing, God will unite Himself, with His greatness. . . . Since it was He who paid the highest price, His Majesty wants to join our little labors with the great ones He suffered so that all the work may become one. (2:343)

Briefly, in one way or another, there must be a cross while we live. (2:345)

Fix your eyes on the Crucified and everything will become small for you. (2:446)

But during the little while this life lasts—and perhaps it will last a shorter time than each one thinks—let us offer the Lord interiorly and exteriorly the sacrifice we can. His Majesty will join it with that which He offered on the cross to the Father for us. Thus even though our works are small they will have the value our love for Him would have merited had they been great. (2:450)

O my Lord, what power over You a sigh of sorrow has that comes from the depths of our heart on seeing that it isn't enough that we are in this exile but that we are not even given the chance to be alone enjoying You. (3:123)

Although mortification is very necessary in order that the soul gain freedom and high perfection, it is not accomplished in a short time. Rather, little by little, ... each one according to the spirituality and amount of intelligence God gives. (3:189)

Yet illness does not usually affect me so much when I see that something is for the service of God. (3:287)

THE
GLORIOUS
MYSTERIES

THE FIRST GLORIOUS MYSTERY

THE RESURRECTION OF JESUS FROM THE DEAD

Faith

Blessed are those who have not seen and yet believe.
—John 20:29

The Lord said to me: "Why are you afraid? Do you not know that I am all-powerful? I will fulfill what I have promised." (1:224)

I thought I would be able to serve God much better if I were in good health. This is our mistake: not abandoning ourselves entirely to what the Lord does, for He knows best what is fitting for us. (1:79)

I often thought that St. Peter didn't lose anything when he threw himself into the sea, even though he grew frightened afterward. These first acts of determination are very important. (1:124)

Let us believe that all is for our own greater good. Let His Majesty lead the way along the path He desires. We belong no longer to ourselves but to Him. (1:116)

I must have failed, as it appears to me now, because I did not put all my trust in His Majesty . . . I didn't understand that all is of little benefit if we do not take away completely the trust we have in ourselves and place it in God. (1:100)

God's words cannot fail. (1:96)

God always understands us and is with us. There is no doubt about this understanding and presence. . . . He wants to begin to work in the soul in a special way. (1:135)

It seemed to me that the more the things of faith go beyond what is natural the stronger the faith—and this thought enkindled great devotion in me. Just believing that You are all powerful was enough for me to receive all the grandeurs that You work, and this power, as I say, I never doubted. (1:168)

I write this for the consolation of weak souls like myself that they might never despair or fail to trust in the greatness of God. (1:166)

The Lord helps us, strengthens us, and never fails; He is a true friend. (1:194)

This Lord of ours is the one through whom all blessings come to us. He will teach us these things. In beholding His life we find that He is the best example. (1:194)

In the measure He sees that they receive Him, so He gives and is given. He loves whoever loves Him; how good a beloved! how good a friend! O Lord of my soul, who has the words to explain what You give to those who trust in You! (1:200)

He shows no partiality, He loves everyone. (1:232)

Lord of all the world and of the heavens, of a thousand other worlds and of numberless worlds, and of the heavens that You might create, how the soul understands by the majesty with which You reveal Yourself that it is nothing for You to be Lord of the world! (1:241)

We are given an understanding of how God is powerful, that He can do all things, that He commands all and governs all, and that His love permeates all things. (1:242)

His Majesty sent strength and placed it in the midst of my weakness. (1:307)

A much greater love for and confidence in this Lord began to develop in me when I saw Him as one with whom I could converse so continually. I saw that He was a man, even though He was God.... I can speak with Him as with a friend, even though He is Lord. (1:325)

God's mercy makes me feel safe. Since He has freed me from so many sins, He will not want to let me out of His hands to go astray. (1:333)

I greatly love those who I see are more advanced and who are determined, detached, and courageous.... I think God helps those who set out to do much for Him and that He never fails anyone who trusts Him alone.
(1:375)

One cannot doubt that the Trinity is in our souls by presence, power, and essence. It is an extremely beneficial thing to understand this truth.... God delights to be with souls. (1:413)

Your works are holy, they are just, they are priceless and done with great wisdom, since You, Lord, are wisdom itself.... The intellect cannot reach the sublime grandeurs of its God. (1:443)

I firmly believe You can do what You desire. And the more I hear of Your greater marvels and consider that You can add to them, the more my faith is strengthened; and I believe with greater determination that You will do this. (1:447)

Oh, oh, oh, how little we trust You, Lord! How much greater the riches and treasures You entrusted to us, since after His thirty-three years of great trials and so unbearable and pitiable a death, You have given us Your Son.
(1:457)

I well understand that one must not put limits on God.... His Majesty has the power to do whatever He wants and is eager to do many things for us. (2:421–22)

Faith and the love of pleasing God make possible what to natural reason is not possible. (3:104)

He gives to each person a proper task, one that He sees as appropriate for that person's soul, for the service of the Lord Himself and for the good of neighbor. And if you have done what you can to be prepared, do not fear that your effort will be lost. (2:103)

Draw near, then, to this good Master with strong determination to learn what He teaches you, and His Majesty will so provide that you will turn out to be good disciples. He will not abandon you if you do not abandon Him. (2:137)

You have a good Father, for He gives you the good Jesus. . . . Cast yourselves into His arms. You already know that He will not reject you if you are good daughters. Who, then, would fail to strive so as not to lose such a Father? (2:139–40)

We have heaven within ourselves since the Lord of heaven is there. (2:147)

Consider that Jesus acts here as our ambassador and that He has desired to intervene between us and His Father, and at no small cost of His own. (2:161)

It is possible for God to grant favors—for it seems sometimes we have forgotten about the Lord's ancient mercies. (2:194)

This other love can no longer be doubted since it was shown so openly and with so many sufferings and trials, and with the shedding of blood even to the point of death in order that we might have no doubt about it.
(2:194)

Oh, my Lord, my Mercy, and my Good! And what greater good could I want in this life than to be so close to You, that there be no division between You and me? With this companionship, what can be difficult? What can one not undertake for You, being so closely joined? (2:246)

How appropriate this name, "powerful King," is, for the Lord has no superior, nor will His reign ever end.
(2:251)

His Majesty will give you through other paths what He keeps from you on this one because of what He knows, for His secrets are very hidden; at least what He does will without any doubt be what is most suitable for us. (2:314)

God can do far more and don't turn your attention to whether the ones to whom He grants His favors are good or bad.... With humility and simplicity of heart we should serve and praise Him for His works and marvels.
(2:339)

The Lord knows what He is doing better than [the soul] knows what it is desiring. (2:349)

It does great harm not to believe that God has the power to do things that our intellects do not understand. (2:373)

I consider it better for us to place ourselves in the presence of the Lord and look at His mercy and grandeur and at our own lowliness, and let Him give us what He wants, whether water or dryness. He knows best what is suitable for us. With such an attitude we shall go about refreshed. (2:395)

The Lord Himself says that He is the way; the Lord says also that He is the light and that no one can go to the Father but through Him, and "anyone who sees me sees my Father." (2:400)

But when we ask You for the honor of Your Son, why wouldn't You hear us, eternal Father, for the sake of Him who lost a thousand honors and a thousand lives for You? Not for us, Lord, for we don't deserve it, but for the blood of Your Son and His merits. (2:51)

The safest way is to want only what God wants. He knows more than we ourselves do, and He loves us. Let us place ourselves in His hands so that His will may be done in us, and we cannot err if with a determined will we always maintain this attitude. (2:417)

I trusted that God would take care of things. (3:275)

> Untiring in loving,
> Our God is calling;
> Trusting Him, let us follow. (3:386)

THE SECOND GLORIOUS MYSTERY

THE ASCENSION OF JESUS INTO HEAVEN

Hope

Ask, and it will be given you; seek, and you will find; knock, and it will be opened to you. —Luke 11:9

By these gifts, the Lord gives us the fortitude that by our sins we are losing. If people don't have, along with a living faith, some pledge of the love God has for them, they will not . . . have all the other great virtues that the perfect possess. For our nature is so dead that we go after what we see in the present. (1:27)

I have seen clearly that God does not leave one, even in this life, without a large reward. (1:44)

I often marveled to think of the great goodness of God, and my soul delighted in seeing His amazing magnificence and mercy. May He be blessed by all, for I have seen clearly that He does not fail to repay, even in this life, every good desire. (1:69)

He never tires of giving, nor can He exhaust His mercies. Let us not tire of receiving. (1:172)

If the soul perseveres in prayer, in the midst of the sins, temptations, and failures of a thousand kinds that the devil places in its path, in the end, I hold as certain, the Lord will draw it forth to the harbor of salvation. (1:95–96)

He surpasses reason in bestowing consolation: He comforts here; He gladdens there. (1:106)

Have great confidence, for it is necessary not to hold back one's desires, but to believe in God that if we try we shall little by little, even though it may not be soon, reach the state the saints did with His help. For if they had never determined to desire and seek this state little by little in practice they would never have mounted so high. (1:123)

In seeing You at my side I saw all blessings. (1:194)

If the Lord hadn't favored me so much, I don't know what would have happened to me. . . . Sometimes I found myself in such straits that I didn't know what to do other than raise my eyes to the Lord. (1:245)

Let not these souls become anxious, let them hope in the Lord; through their prayer and their doing what they can, His Majesty will bring it about that what they now have in desires they shall possess in deed. (1:272)

Let us not cease to believe that even in this life God gives the hundredfold. (1:46)

I don't see, Lord, nor do I know how the road that leads to You is narrow. I see that it is a royal road, not a path; a road that is safer for anyone who indeed takes it. (1:308)

He is always present giving us being. (1:356)

I have seen clearly that ... here on earth the Lord has no measure in giving when He is pleased to do so. Thus I wouldn't want to use any measure in my service to His Majesty and in employing all my life and strength and health to this end. (1:323)

I found myself so constricted on every side that the only remedy I discovered was to raise my eyes to heaven and call upon God.... For there is no stable help but in God. (1:350)

He [Jesus] told me with much love that I shouldn't be anxious, that in this life we cannot always be in a stable condition, that sometimes the soul will experience fervor and at other times be without it, that sometimes it will have disturbances and at other times have quiet, and again temptations; but that it should hope in Him and not be afraid. (1:360)

I have experience that the true remedy against a fall is to be attached to the cross and trust in Him who placed Himself upon it. (1:382)

You, my Lord and my delight, knowing the many needs there must be and the comfort it is for us to rely on You, tell us to ask You and that You will not fail to give. (1:447)

When I consider how You say that Your delights are with the children of the earth, my soul rejoices greatly. O Lord of heaven and earth, what words these are that no sinner might be wanting in trust! (1:449)

You say: *Come to me all who labor and are burdened, for I will comfort you.* What more do we want, Lord? What are we asking for? What do we seek? Why are those in the world so unhappy if not because of seeking rest? (1:450)

Open your eyes, with loud cries and tears seek light from the one who gave it to the world. (1:455)

Life lasts but a couple of hours; exceedingly great will be the reward. If we should do nothing else but what the Lord counseled us to do, the pay of just being able in some way to imitate Him would be great. (2:46)

He is so good. . . . He gives drink to those who wish to follow Him so that no one will go without consolation or die of thirst. Rivers stream from this overflowing fount.
(2:114)

Good never produces evil. (2:115)

In taking account of us, He is not at all petty, but generous. . . . Just the raising of our eyes in remembrance of Him will have its reward. (2:126)

The Majesty! How victorious! How joyful! Indeed, like one coming forth from a battle where he has gained a great kingdom! And all of that, plus Himself, He desires for you. Well, is it such a big thing that from time to time you turn your eyes to look upon one who gives you so much? (2:134)

He must be better than all the fathers in the world because in Him everything must be faultless. And after all this He must make us sharers and heirs with You.
(2:138)

You have spoken, as a favored son, for Yourself and for us; and You are powerful enough so that what You say on earth will be done in heaven. . . . You are so willing to give that nothing will stop You from doing so. (2:138–39)

His Majesty never tires of giving. (2:164)

Consider what you have given as very little since you will receive so much. (2:166)

He likes us to be truthful with Him. If we speak plainly and clearly so that we don't say one thing and then act differently, He always gives more than what we ask of Him. (2:184)

What does it cost us to ask for a great deal? We are asking it of One who is powerful. But in order to be right, let us leave the giving to His will since we have already given Him our own. (2:202–3)

Oh, Christians and my daughters! Let us now, for love of the Lord, awake from this sleep and behold that He does not keep the reward of loving Him for the next life alone. The pay begins in this life. O my Jesus, who could explain the benefit that lies in throwing ourselves into the arms of this Lord of ours! (2:246)

Our most sacred King has still much to give. He would never want to do anything else than give if He could find receivers. And as I have said often—I want you never to forget, daughters—the Lord is never content with giving us as little as we desire. (2:250–51)

God doesn't like us to put a limit on His works. (2:285)

I don't find anything comparable to the magnificent beauty of a soul and its marvelous capacity. Indeed, our intellects, however keen, can hardly comprehend it.... He created us in His own image and likeness. (2:283)

Isn't it clear that the soul to whom God grants so great a favor as to join it with Himself in a friendship like this will be left truly rich in His blessings? (2:240)

If you should at times fall don't become discouraged and stop striving to advance. For even from this fall God will draw out good. (2:302)

To the little we do, which is nothing, God will unite Himself, with His greatness, and give it such high value that the Lord Himself will become the reward of this work. (2:343)

Everything that there is in this great God is magnificent. (2:382)

He doesn't desire anything else than to have those to whom to give. His riches do not lessen when He gives them away. (2:383–84)

And if they do not see what is now seen, let them not blame the times, for it is always a suitable time for God to grant great favors to the one who truly serves Him. (3:115)

Although God also gives these other virtues, they can in addition be the objects of our striving. . . . May His Majesty give them to us since no one who strives for them with effort, solicitude, prayer, and confidence in His mercy will be denied by Him. (3:143)

I hope in the goodness of God that He will be merciful to us at the moment of death through the merits of His Son and those of His glorious Mother. (3:178)

May He be blessed and praised for everything. For He repays our lowly deeds with eternal life and glory, and He makes them great while they are in fact of little value. (3:147)

The Third Glorious Mystery

The Descent of the Holy Spirit

Love of God

You shall love the Lord your God with all your heart, and with all your soul, and with all your mind, and with all your strength.—Mark 12:30

Prayer is an exercise of love. (1:88)

I liked images so much. Unfortunate are those who through their own fault lose this great good. It indeed appears that they do not love the Lord, for if they loved Him they would rejoice to see a portrait of Him, just as here on earth it really gives joy to see one whom you deeply love. (1:102)

The love of God does not consist in tears or in this delight and tenderness, which for the greater part we desire and find consolation in; but it consists in serving with justice and fortitude of soul and in humility. Without such service it seems to me we would be receiving everything and giving nothing. (1:117)

It is very obvious that we love others more when we often recall the good works they do for us. . . . Keep always in mind that we have our being from God, that He created us from nothing and sustains us, and all the other benefits flowing from His death and trials. (1:107)

What a charming way to seek the love of God! (1:111)

The perfect attainment of this true love of God brings with it every blessing. . . . There is nothing on earth with which one can buy so wonderful a blessing. (1:111)

The soul is therefore neither content with nor desirous of the world's satisfactions, because it has in itself what pleases it more . . . [a] desire to enjoy Him more and to be with Him. Being with Him is what it wants. (1:154)

As often as we think of Christ we should recall the love with which He bestowed on us so many favors and what great love God showed us in giving us a pledge like this of His love, for love begets love. (1:198)

Let us strive to keep this divine love always before our eyes and to waken ourselves to love. If at some time the Lord should favor us by impressing this love on our hearts, all will become easy for us, and we shall carry out our tasks quickly and without much effort. (1:198)

Oh, how many times do I recall the living water that the Lord told the Samaritan woman about! And so I am very fond of that gospel passage. . . . I often begged the Lord to give me the water. I always carried with me a painting of this episode of the Lord at the well. (1:262–63)

❦

I see that whoever understands Him more loves and praises Him more. (1:324)

Consider the Lord as very deep within [your soul]; such a thought is much more alluring and fruitful than thinking of Him as outside oneself. (1:356)

It seemed to me there came the thought of how a sponge absorbs and is saturated with water; so, I thought, was my soul which was overflowing with that divinity and in a certain way rejoicing within itself and possessing the three Persons. (1:392)

Love alone is what gives value to all things; and a kind of love so great that nothing hinders it is the one thing necessary. But how can we possess, my God, a love in conformity with what the Beloved deserves, if Your love does not join love with itself? (1:448)

I have always seen in my God much greater and more extraordinary signs of love than I have known how to ask for or desire! . . . My God, give to me what I might give to you, as St. Augustine says, so that I may repay You something of the great debt I owe You. (1:448)

I desire nothing but to love You. (1:448)

Virtue always inspires love. (2:56)

These souls are more inclined to give than to receive. Even with respect to the Creator Himself they want to give more than to receive. I say that this attitude is what merits the name "love". (2:64)

Behold it is a beautiful exchange to give our love for His. Consider that He can do all things, and we can't do anything here below but what He enables us to do. (2:97)

Consider that it is well worthwhile for you to have understood this truth: that the Lord is within us, and that there we must be with Him. (2:141)

This little heaven of our soul [is] where the Maker of heaven and earth is present. (2:142)

The Lord goes in search of those who do love Him so as to give more to them. (2:159)

What we can have, daughters, and what His Majesty gave us are love and fear. Love will quicken our steps; fear will make us watch our steps to avoid falling along the way. . . . What more could you ask for! They are like two fortified castles from which one can wage war on the world and the devils. (2:192)

If we possess love, we are certainly in the state of grace. (2:192)

Those who truly love God, love every good, desire every good, favor every good, praise every good. They always join, favor, and defend good people. They have no love for anything but truth and whatever is worthy of love. (2:192)

The love makes itself known according to its intensity. When slight, it shows itself but slightly; when strong, it shows itself strongly. But where there is love of God, whether little or great, it is always recognized. (2:193)

In this love—besides everything else—there is greater security than with earthly loves; in loving God we are certain that He loves us. Remember here, my daughters, the gain there is in this love, and the loss in not having it. (2:195)

You have a Lord and Spouse with whom nothing takes place without His seeing and understanding it! Thus, even though the things be very small, do not fail to do what you can for love of Him. His Majesty will repay for them; He looks only at the love with which you do them. (2:218)

It seems to me that love is like an arrow sent forth by the will. If it travels with all the force that the will has, freed from all earthly things, and directed to God alone, it truly must wound His Majesty. (2:252)

Well, let us imagine that within us is an extremely rich palace, built entirely of gold and precious stones; in sum, built for a Lord such as this.... Imagine, also, that in this palace dwells this mighty King. (2:268)

The important thing is not to think much but to love much; and so do that which best stirs you to love. (2:272)

The Lord doesn't look so much at the greatness of our works as at the love with which they are done.... Thus even though our works are small they will have the value our love for Him would have merited had they been great. (2:278)

Come to love a goodness so perfect and a mercy so immeasurable. (2:285)

This Lord desires intensely that we love Him and seek His company, so much so that from time to time He calls us to draw near Him. And His voice is so sweet.... They come through words spoken by other good people, or through sermons, or through what is read in good books, or through the many things that are heard and by which God calls. (2:298)

He must give the reward in conformity with the love we have for Him. And this love, daughters, must not be fabricated in our imaginations but proved by deeds. And don't think He needs our works; He needs the determination of our wills. (2:308)

Rather, as one who has received more, you are more indebted. What can we do for a God so generous that He died for us, created us, and gives us being? (2:308)

It is love's nature to serve with deeds in a thousand ways. (2:418)

Love increases in the measure the soul discovers how much this great God and Lord deserves to be loved. (2:421)

Just as a great gush of water could not reach us if it didn't have a source, as I have said, so it is understood clearly that there is Someone in the interior depths who shoots these arrows and gives life to this life, and that there is a Sun in the interior of the soul from which a brilliant light proceeds. (2:435)

If you do not strive for the virtues and practice them, you will always be dwarfs. . . . Whoever does not increase decreases. I hold that love, where present, cannot possibly be content with remaining always the same. (2:447)

All souls are capable of loving. . . . The soul's progress does not lie in thinking much but in loving much. (3:117)

The true lover loves everywhere. (3:123)

Love has this strength if it is perfect, for we forget about pleasing ourselves in order to please the one we love. And truly this is so; for even though the trials may be very great, they become sweet when we know we are pleasing God. (3:120)

Much more can be merited by making an act of love and by often awakening the will to greater love of God than by leaving it listless. (3:125–26)

The smallest thing when done for the love of God is priceless. (3:159)

The Fourth Glorious Mystery

The Assumption of Mary into Heaven

Desire for Heaven

Come, O blessed of my Father, inherit the kingdom prepared for you from the foundation of the world.—Matthew 25:34

His goodness will make [the soul] a citizen of heaven, provided it doesn't stop through its own fault; and unhappy it will be if it turns back. (1:140)

We should fix our eyes on the true and everlasting kingdom which we are trying to gain. It is very important to keep this kingdom always in mind. (1:145)

Glorified bodies have such beauty. (1:237)

Nor is the soul content with less than God. (1:252)

When, my God, will I finally see my soul joined together in Your praise, so that all its faculties may enjoy You? (1:261)

It is right for anyone who cares about heaven to have a continual solicitude about pleasing God. (1:328)

These revelations also helped me very much, I think, in coming to know our true country and realizing that we are pilgrims here below; it is a wonderful thing to see what is there and know where we shall live. (1:332)

Merely to look toward heaven recollects the soul. (1:332)

If someone has to go to live permanently in another country, it is a great help to them in undergoing the struggle of the journey to have seen that it is a land where they will be very much at ease. (1:332)

I am consoled to hear the clock strike, for at the passing away of that hour of life it seems to me I am drawing a little closer to the vision of God. (1:361)

O death, death, I don't know who fears you, since life lies in you! (1:449)

May You be blessed, my God, forever! May all things praise You, Lord, without end since in You there can be no end.... O Lord, my God, how You possess the words of eternal life, where all mortals will find what they desire if they want to seek it! (1:450)

Why don't you want to live forever? Oh, hardness of human hearts! May Your boundless compassion, my God, soften these hearts. (1:453)

If when something is lost . . . we feel sad, why don't we feel sad upon losing this royal eagle of God's majesty and a kingdom of endless enjoyment? What is this? I don't understand it. My God, cure such a great foolishness and blindness. (1:458)

Short is all life in exchange for Your eternity. (1:462)

Oh, when will that happy day arrive when you will see yourself drowned in the infinite sea of supreme truth, where you will no longer be free to sin! Nor will you want to sin, for you will be safe from every misery, naturalized by the life of your God! (1:462–63)

Then, my soul, you will enter into your rest when you become intimate with this supreme Good, understand what He understands, love what He loves, and rejoice in what gives Him joy. (1:463)

It would be a good exchange to give up everything for the enjoyment of everlasting abundance. (2:44)

The Lord should lead you in such a way that you are left with some thirst in this life, in the life that lasts forever He will give you to drink in great plenty and you will have no fear of being without water. (2:114)

Do not be frightened, daughters, by the many things you need to consider in order to begin this divine journey which is the royal road to heaven. A great treasure is gained by traveling this road; no wonder we have to pay what seems to us a high price. The time will come when you will understand how trifling everything is next to so precious a reward. (2:117)

You are a King forever, my God; Your kingdom is not a borrowed one. When in the Creed the words "and His kingdom will have no end" are said, it is almost always a special delight for me. (2:122)

The great good that it seems to me there will be in the kingdom of heaven, among many other blessings, is that one will no longer take any account of earthly things, but have a calmness and glory within, rejoice in the fact that all are rejoicing, experience perpetual peace and a wonderful inner satisfaction that comes from seeing that everyone hallows and praises the Lord. (2:151)

Let us always direct our thoughts to what is lasting. (2:146)

Everyone loves Him there, and the soul itself doesn't think about anything else than loving Him; nor can it cease loving Him, because it knows Him. (2:151)

It is no surprise that those who have a share in the consolations of God desire to be there where they will enjoy them more than in mere sips. . . . They desire to be where the Sun of justice does not set. (2:202)

He wants us to desire the eternal; we, here below, lean toward what comes to an end. He wants us to desire sublime and great things; we, here below, desire base and earthly things. He would want us to desire only what is secure; we, here below, love the dubious. (2:202)

I say that the blessedness we must ask for is that of being already secure with the blessed. (2:305)

Through His favors we can understand something of what He will give us in heaven without the intervals, trials, and dangers that there are in this tempestuous sea.
(2:358)

What can give us greater happiness? (2:397)

Little can be known here below with certitude; we must wait until the true Judge gives to each one what is merited. In heaven we will be surprised to see how different His judgment is from what we can understand here below. (2:410)

The Lord's presence is the most beautiful and delightful a person could imagine even were he to live and labor a thousand years thinking about it (for it far surpasses the limitations of our imagination or intellect.)
(2:412)

It also seems to me that the soul and the faculties are not one but different. There are so many and such delicate things in the interior that it would be boldness on my part to set out to explain them. In heaven we will see all this. (2:432)

In the final analysis, by proceeding with humility, through the mercy of God, we will reach that city of Jerusalem, where all that has been suffered will be little, or nothing, in comparison with what is enjoyed. (3:114)

Let us praise Him, my Sisters. . . . Let us not tire of praising so great a King and Lord, who has prepared for us a kingdom without end in exchange for some little troubles which will end tomorrow and which come wrapped in a thousand joys. (3:306)

> That life from above,
> That is true life. . . .
> Death, be not aloof;
> In dying first, may life be,
> *I die because I do not die.* (3:376)

> In You alone, Sovereign Majesty,
> I find my peace. (3:378)

The Fifth Glorious Mystery

The Crowning of Mary Queen
of Heaven and Earth

Devotion to Mary

Behold, your Mother!
—John 19:27

I sought out solitude to pray my devotions, and they were many, especially the rosary, to which my mother was very devoted; and she made us devoted to it too. (1:55–56)

I remember that when my mother died I was twelve years old. . . . When I began to understand what I had lost, I went, afflicted, before an image of our Lady and besought her with many tears to be my mother. It seems to me that although I did this in simplicity it helped me. (1:56)

I have found favor with this sovereign Virgin in everything I have asked of her, and in the end she has drawn me to herself. (1:56)

To see a work accomplished that I knew was for the service of the Lord and to the honor of the habit of His glorious Mother—these were my concerns. (1:311)

I prayed very much [to St. Joseph], as I did also to our Lady. (1:256)

I saw our Lady in the greatest glory clothed in a white mantle; it seemed she was sheltering us all under it. I understood how high a degree of glory the Lord would give to those living in this house. (1:320)

I was left with a longing to serve our Lady since she deserved this so much. (1:353)

He showed me [His Mother's] ascent to heaven, the happiness and solemnity with which she was received, and the place where she is. . . . The glory my spirit experienced in seeing so much glory was magnificent. The effects of this favor were great. (1:353)

[Jesus] told me that immediately after His resurrection He went to see our Lady because she then had great need and that the pain she experienced so absorbed and transpierced her soul that she did not return immediately to herself to rejoice in that joy. . . . What must have been that transpiercing of the Blessed Virgin's soul! (1:390–91)

I saw Christ who seemed to be receiving me with great love and placing a crown on my head and thanking me for what I did for His Mother. (1:320)

He told me: "I gave you My Son, and the Holy Spirit, and this Blessed Virgin. What can you give Me?" (1:396)

I understood that I had a great obligation to serve our Lady and St. Joseph; for often when I went off the path completely, God gave me salvation again through their prayers. (1:399)

On another day the Lord told me this: "Do you think, daughter, that merit lies in enjoyment? No, rather it lies in working and suffering and loving. . . . When you see My Mother holding Me in her arms, don't think she enjoyed those consolations without heavy torment. From the time Simeon spoke those words to her, My Father gave her clear light to see what I was to suffer." (1:403)

The beauty I saw in our Lady was extraordinary. (1:291)

I saw the Mother of God descend with a great multitude of angels and sit in the prioress's choir stall where there was a statue of our Lady. . . . She told me: "You were indeed right in placing me here; I shall be present in the praises they give my Son, and I shall offer these praises to Him." (1:395)

If there should be anything good in this work, may it be for the honor and glory of God and the service of His most Blessed Mother, our Lady and Patroness, whose habit I wear. (2:38)

What a marvelous thing, that He who would fill a thousand worlds and many more with His grandeur would enclose Himself in something so small! And so He wanted to enclose Himself in the womb of His most Blessed Mother. (2:144)

If only they [some learned men] could learn something from the humility of the most Blessed Virgin! (2:211)

With greater reason might He have complained to His Mother and our Lady when she was at the foot of the cross, and not asleep but suffering in her most holy soul and dying a harsh death; it always consoles us more to complain to those who we know feel our trials and love us more. (2:241)

[Souls easily conquered] must take His Blessed Mother and His saints as intercessors so that these intercessors may fight for them. (2:293)

In spite of all her wisdom she asked the angel: *How can this be?* But after he answered, *The Holy Spirit will come upon you; the power of the Most High will overshadow you,* she engaged in no further discussion. As one who had such great faith and wisdom, she understood at once that if these two intervened, there was nothing more to know or doubt. (2:253)

I can boast only of His mercy, and since I cannot cease being what I have been, I have no other remedy than to approach His mercy and to trust in the merits of His Son and of the Virgin, His Mother. (2:305)

You have such a good Mother. Imitate her and reflect that the grandeur of our Lady and the good of having her for your patroness must be indeed great. (2:305–6)

Jesus is too good a companion for us to turn away from Him and His most blessed Mother. (2:403)

She was firm in the faith; she knew He was God and man, and even though she loved Him more than [the disciples] did, she did so with such perfection. (2:404)

It is important to know that our Lord is pleased with any service rendered to His Mother, and great is His mercy. (3:147)

It is her custom to favor those who want to be protected by her. (3:218)

We were happy to be able to serve in some way our Mother, Lady, and Patroness. (3:276)

She is our Lady and our Patroness. And this for me was one of the great joys and satisfactions of my life. (3:279)

> Let us go to the shepherdess. . . .
> Is she a relative of the Mayor,
> Or who is this maiden?
> God the Father's daughter,
> Glowing starlike. (3:391)

OTHER
TOPICS

PRAYER

❧

Watch and pray that you may not enter into temptation.
— Mark 14:38

I say only that prayer is the door to favors as great as those He granted me. If this door is closed, I don't know how He will grant them. (1:46)

Prayer is an exercise of love, and it would be incorrect to think that if there is no time for solitude there is no prayer at all. With a little care great blessings can come when because of our labors the Lord takes from us the time we had set for prayer. (1:88)

Great good God does for a soul that willingly disposes itself for the practice of prayer, even though it is not as disposed as is necessary. . . . The good that one who practices prayer possesses has been written of by many saints and holy persons. (1:95–96)

No one can truly discover any harm that prayer can do—the greatest harm being not to practice it—why do those who serve God and desire to serve Him abandon it? (1:98)

It seemed to me that in this life there could be no greater good than the practice of prayer. (1:87)

This prayer, then, is a little spark of the Lord's true love which He begins to enkindle in the soul; and He desires that the soul grow in the understanding of what this love accompanied by delight is. (1:141)

Whether we like it or not, my daughters, we must all journey toward this fount, even though in different ways. Well, believe me; and don't let anyone deceive you by showing you a road other than that of prayer. (2:119)

I say that should anyone have some doubt little would be lost in trying the journey of prayer; for this journey brings with it the following good: more is given than is asked for, beyond what we could desire. This is absolutely true. (2:128)

Souls who practice prayer walk so much more securely than those who take another road. They are like those in the stands watching the bull in comparison with one who is right in front of its horns. (2:191)

I tried as hard as I could to keep Jesus Christ, our God and our Lord, present within me, and that was my way of prayer. If I reflected upon some phrase of His Passion, I represented Him to myself interiorly. (1:67)

Reading is very helpful for recollection and serves as a necessary substitute—even though little may be read—for anyone who is unable to practice mental prayer. (1:68)

I would counsel those who practice prayer to seek, at least in the beginning, friendship and association with other persons having the same interest. This is something most important even though the association may be only to help one another with prayers. (1:92)

Is it too much to ask you to turn your eyes from these exterior things in order to look at Him sometimes? Behold, He is not waiting for anything else, as He says to the bride, than that we look at Him. In the measure you desire Him, you will find Him. (2:134)

It seemed to me that Jesus Christ was always present at my side. . . . He was the witness of everything I did. At no time in which I was a little recollected, or not greatly distracted, was I able to ignore He was present at my side. (1:228)

Since you speak with other persons, why must words fail you more when you speak with God? Don't believe they will; at least I will not believe they will if you acquire the habit. (2:136)

Who can keep you from turning the eyes of your soul toward this Lord? (2:32)

I began to practice prayer without knowing what it was; and the custom became so habitual that I did not abandon it, just as I did not fail to make the sign of the cross before sleeping. (1:102)

Those who follow this path of no discursive reflection will find that a book can be a help for recollecting oneself quickly. It helped me also to look at fields, or water, or flowers. In these things I found a remembrance of the Creator. (1:102)

I strove to recollect myself in His presence. This is a pleasing prayer, if God helps in it, and the delight is great. (1:192)

The Our Father and the Hail Mary are sufficient. (2:25)

Silence is better observed when each nun is by herself; and to get used to solitude is a great help for prayer. (2:27)

Speak with Him as with a father, or a brother, or a lord, or as with a spouse; sometimes in one way, at other times in another; He will teach you what you must do in order to please Him. (2:141)

I'm not asking you now that you think about Him or that you draw out a lot of concepts or make long and subtle reflections with your intellect. I'm not asking you to do anything more than look at Him. (2:32)

It is always good to base your prayer on prayers coming from the mouth of the Lord. (2:118)

We must, then, disengage ourselves from everything so as to approach God interiorly and even in the midst of occupations withdraw within ourselves. Although it may be for only a moment that I remember I have that Company within myself, doing so is very beneficial. (2:147)

Since vocal prayer is prayer it must be accompanied by reflection. A prayer in which a person is not aware of whom he is speaking to, what he is asking, who it is who is asking and of whom, I do not call prayer however much the lips move. (2:286)

I know there are many persons who while praying vocally, as has been already mentioned, are raised by God to sublime contemplation. (2:33)

Certainly, it never entered my mind that this prayer [Our Father] contained so many deep secrets; for now you have seen the entire spiritual way contained in it, from the beginning stages until God engulfs the soul and gives it to drink abundantly from the fount of living water. (2:34)

If while speaking I thoroughly understand and know that I am speaking with God and I have greater awareness of this than I do of the words I'm saying, mental and vocal prayer are joined. (2:121)

When I say, "I believe," it seems to me right that I should know and understand what I believe. And when I say, "Our Father," it will be an act of love to understand who this Father of ours is and who the Master is who taught us this prayer. (2:129)

The teacher is never so far from his pupil that he has to shout, but he is very close. I want you to understand that it is good for you, if you are to recite the Our Father well, to remain at the side of the Master who taught this prayer to you. (2:130)

To recite the Our Father or the Hail Mary or whatever prayer you wish is vocal prayer. But behold what poor music you produce when you do this without mental prayer. (2:132)

It may seem to anyone who doesn't know about the matter that vocal prayer doesn't go with contemplation; but I know that it does.... It's because of this that I insist so much, daughters, upon your reciting vocal prayer well. (2:152)

You do much more by saying one word of the Our Father from time to time than by rushing through the entire prayer many times. You are very close to the One you petition; He will not fail to hear you. And believe that herein lies the true praise and hallowing of His name. (2:159)

One should not always weary oneself in seeking these reflections but just remain there in His presence with the intellect quiet. And if we are able we should occupy ourselves in looking at Christ who is looking at us. (1:28)

Mental prayer in my opinion is nothing else than an intimate sharing between friends; it means taking time frequently to be alone with Him who we know loves us. In order that love be true and friendship endure, the wills of the friends must be in accord. (1:96)

I strove to represent Christ within me, and it did me greater good—in my opinion—to represent Him in those scenes where I saw Him more alone. It seemed to me that being alone and afflicted, as a person in need, He had to accept me. (1:101)

Let us begin to think about an episode of the Passion, let's say of when our Lord was bound to the pillar. . . . This is the method of prayer with which all must begin, continue, and finish; and it is a very excellent and safe path until the Lord leads one to other supernatural things. (1:129)

We are very near His Majesty. . . . Ask for His gifts and pray for the Church and for those who have asked for our prayers and for the souls in purgatory, not with the noise of words but with longing that He hear us. (1:142)

This prayer of quiet is the beginning of all blessings. (1:146–47)

Therefore, Sisters, out of love for the Lord, get used to praying the Our Father with this recollection, and you will see the benefit before long. This is a manner of praying that the soul gets so quickly used to that it doesn't go astray, nor do the faculties become restless, as time will tell. (2:33)

Let us give ourselves to mental prayer. And let whoever cannot practice it turn to vocal prayer, reading, and colloquy with God. (2:103)

Do you think He is silent? Even though we do not hear Him, He speaks well to the heart when we beseech Him from the heart. (2:130)

I don't know how mental prayer can be separated from vocal prayer if the vocal prayer is to be recited well with an understanding of whom we are speaking to. . . . The best remedy I find is to strive to center the mind upon the one to whom the words are addressed. (2:130)

I'm not asking you to do anything more than look at Him. For who can keep you from turning the eyes of your soul toward this Lord, even if you do so just for a moment if you can't do more? (2:134)

In spite of any wrong they who practice prayer do, they must not abandon prayer since it is the means by which they can remedy the situation; and to remedy it without prayer would be much more difficult. (1:96)

The soul is capable of much more than we can imagine, and the sun that is in this royal chamber shines in all parts. It is very important for any soul that practices prayer, whether little or much, not to hold itself back and stay in one corner. (2:291)

We begin to think about the favor God granted us in giving us His only Son, and we do not stop there, but go on to the mysteries of His whole glorious life. . . . This kind of reflection is an admirable and very meritorious prayer. (2:401–2)

Return to the search for God by means of a friendship as special as is that found in the intimate exchange of prayer. (1:82)

What I advise strongly is not to abandon prayer, for in prayer people will understand what they are doing and win repentance from the Lord and fortitude to lift themselves up. (1:140)

You must believe that if you give up prayer, you are, in my opinion, courting danger. (1:140)

I saw that I was increasing very much in His love. I went to Him to complain about all these trials, and I always came away from prayer consoled and with new strength. (1:247–48)

Be extremely careful for the love of the Lord not to be tricked into giving up prayer. (1:171)

Prayer is a safe road; you will be more quickly freed from temptation when close to the Lord than when far. (2:192)

It is in the effects and deeds following afterward that one discerns the true value of prayer. (2:273)

[Prayer] is the place where the Lord gives the light to understand truths. (3:150)

He teaches during the brief moments we spend in prayer; however lukewarm these moments may be, God esteems them highly. (2:298)

It is not the length of time spent in prayer that benefits one; when the time is spent as well in good works, it is a great help in preparing the soul for the enkindling of love. The soul may thereby be better prepared in a very short time than through many hours of reflection. (3:123)

Though we are always in the presence of God, it seems to me the manner is different with those who practice prayer, for they are aware that He is looking at them. With others, it can happen that several days pass without their recalling that God sees them. (1:95)

THE EUCHARIST

He who eats my flesh and drinks my blood has eternal life, and I will raise him up at the last day.—John 6:54

After having received Communion ... the Lord spoke these words to me: "It [the soul] detaches itself from everything, daughter, so as to abide more in me. It is no longer the soul that lives but I." (1:163)

I cannot say this without tears and great joy of soul! How You desire, Lord, thus to be with us and to be present in the Sacrament.... You would be glad to be with us since You say that Your delight is to be with children of the earth. (1:138)

I always returned to my custom of rejoicing in this Lord, especially when I received Communion. I wanted to keep ever before my eyes a painting or image of Him since I was unable to keep Him as engraved in my soul as I desired. (1:192)

We have Him so near in the Blessed Sacrament, where He is already glorified. (1:193)

Corpus Christi [is] a feast for which I have much devotion. (1:258)

Behold Him here without suffering, full of glory, before ascending into heaven, strengthening some, encouraging others, our companion in the most Blessed Sacrament; it doesn't seem it was in His power to leave us for even a moment. (1:193)

Sometimes ... after receiving Communion I was at peace. And sometimes in approaching the Sacrament I felt at once so good in soul and body that I was surprised. It seems that in only a moment all the darknesses of the soul disperse. (1:260)

When I approached to receive Communion and recalled the extraordinary majesty I had seen and considered that it was present in the Blessed Sacrament (the Lord often desires that I behold it in the host), ... the whole experience seemed to annihilate me. (1:337)

O Wealth of the poor, how admirably You know how to sustain souls! ... When I behold majesty as extraordinary as this concealed in something as small as the host, it happens afterward that I marvel at wisdom so wonderful. (1:337)

Understand the power of the words of consecration and how God does not fail to be present, ... all out of love for me and for everyone. (1:338–39)

I understood well how much more priests are obliged to be good than are others, how deplorable a thing it is to receive this most Blessed Sacrament unworthily. (1:339)

On occasion there come over me such ardent desires to receive Communion that I don't think they could be exaggerated. (1:351)

From certain things He told me, I understood that after He ascended to heaven He never came down to earth to commune with anyone except in the most Blessed Sacrament. (1:390)

One day after having received Communion, I truly thought my soul was made one with the most sacred Body of the Lord. He appeared to me and by His presence caused me to make much progress. (1:411)

Once after receiving Communion I was given understanding of how the Father receives within our soul the most holy Body of Christ, and of how I know and have seen that these divine Persons are present, and of how pleasing to the Father this offering of His Son is. (1:414)

I was already so outside myself with the desire for Communion that even should lances have been held to my heart I think I'd have gone into their midst. (1:351)

It's as though Jesus tells the Father that He is now ours since the Father has given Him to us to die for us; and asks that the Father not take Him from us until the end of the world; that He allow Him to serve each day. (2:167–68)

He realizes that we are weak and knows that the laborers must be nourished with such food. (2:51)

In this petition [Our Father] the word "daily" seems to mean forever.... I've come to think that it is because here on earth we possess Him and also in heaven we will possess Him if we profit well by His company. He, in fact, doesn't remain with us for any other reason than to help, encourage, and sustain us. (2:168)

In no matter how many ways the soul may desire to eat, it will find delight and consolation in the most Blessed Sacrament. (2:169)

Do you think this heavenly food fails to provide sustenance, even for these bodies, that it is not a great medicine even for bodily ills? I know that it is.... The wonders this most sacred bread effects in those who worthily receive it are well known. (2:171)

Receiving Communion is not like picturing with the imagination, as when we reflect upon the Lord on the cross or in other episodes of the Passion, when we picture within ourselves how things happened to Him in the past. In Communion the event is happening now, and it is entirely true. (2:172)

There's no reason to go looking for Him in some other place farther away. (2:172)

If when He went about in the world the mere touch of His robes cured the sick, why doubt, if we have faith, that miracles will be worked while He is within us and that He will give what we ask of Him, since He is in our house? (2:172)

His Majesty is not accustomed to paying poorly for His lodging if the hospitality is good. (2:172)

Be with Him willingly; don't lose so good an occasion for conversing with Him as is the hour after having received Communion. (2:173)

If you immediately turn your thoughts to other things, if you pay no attention and take no account of the fact that He is within you, how will He be able to reveal Himself to you? This, then, is a good time for our Master to teach us, and for us to listen to Him. (2:173)

After having received the Lord, since you have the Person Himself present, strive to close the eyes of the body and open those of the soul and look into your own heart.... You should acquire the habit of doing this every time you receive Communion. (2:173)

Spiritual communion is highly beneficial; through it you can recollect yourselves in the same way after Mass, for the love of this Lord is thereby deeply impressed on the soul. (2:174)

Though He comes disguised, the disguise, as I have said, does not prevent Him from being recognized in many ways, in conformity with the desire we have to see Him. And you can desire to see Him so much that He will reveal Himself to you entirely. (2:173)

The devil will make you think you find more devotion in other things and less in this recollection after Communion. Do not abandon this practice; the Lord will see in it how much you love Him. (2:175)

Certainly, I think that if we were to approach the most Blessed Sacrament with great faith and love, once would be enough to leave us rich. How much richer from approaching so many times as we do. The trouble is we do so out of routine, and it shows. (2:241)

You are mine. . . . You came into the world for me; for me You underwent severe trials; for me You suffered many lashes; for me You remain in the most Blessed Sacrament. (2:246)

We took the Blessed Sacrament and had it reserved in the church with great and well-organized solemnity. It caused much devotion. (3:278)

One day, while I was hearing Mass, at the elevation of the host, I saw Christ on the cross. He spoke some words of consolation. . . . And everything came about afterward as the Lord had told me. (1:335)

CONFESSION

❦

Receive the Holy Spirit. If you forgive the sins of any, they are forgiven; if you retain the sins of any, they are retained.
—John 20:22–23

I hastened to go to confession, for I always liked to confess frequently. (1:75)

For among other favors His Majesty has given me since my first Communion, there is this one: that I never fail to confess what I think is a sin even though venial. (1:75)

I saw the wonderful favor the Lord bestowed in giving me these tears and such deep repentance. I endeavored to go to confession right away and, in my opinion, I did what I could to return to God's grace. (1:78)

O my Jesus! What a sight it is when You through Your mercy return to offer Your hand and raise up a soul that has fallen in sin. . . . You have left such a medicine and ointment for our wounds and because this medicine not only covers these wounds but takes them away completely. (1:166–67)

I talked with my confessor; he always consoled me greatly when he saw that I was troubled. (1:248)

Praised be the Lord who has given me the grace to obey my confessors, even though imperfectly. (1:208)

In similar cases and others as well, in which the devil could ensnare one in many difficulties and in which one does not know what counsel to take, the best thing to do is try to speak with some learned person. . . . Make your confession to him and do what he tells you to do about the matter. (2:57)

Always strive, O daughters, so that you don't go to the confessor each time to confess the same fault. (2:230)

I know that the Lord Himself who walks with you will console you, assure you, and give the confessor light that he may give it to you. (2:409)

I beg the Lord to give my confessors light in conformity with what they can know naturally. And when His Majesty wants something to be done, He puts it in their heart. This has happened to me many times. (3:180)

Since I believe that my confessors stand so truly in the place of God, I think they are the ones for whom I feel the most benevolence. (1:325)

THE CHURCH

So now I say to you: You are Peter and on this rock I will build my Church. And the gates of the underworld can never hold out against it.—Matthew 16:18

In all that I say in this book I submit to what our Mother the Holy Roman Catholic Church holds. If there should be anything contrary to that, it will be due to my not understanding the matter. (2:38)

[With a] strong living faith . . . [the soul] always strives to proceed in conformity with what the Church holds. . . . All the revelations [a soul] could imagine—even if it were to see the heavens open—wouldn't move it one bit from what the Church holds. (1:218)

I don't know why we are amazed that there are so many evils in the Church since those who are to be the models from which all might copy the virtues are so obscurely fashioned that the spirit of the saints of the past has abandoned the religious communities. May it please the divine Majesty to remedy this as He sees it to be necessary. (1:85)

Harm . . . comes to the Church from these heresies that give rise to the loss of so many souls. (1:127)

Our prayer for those who give us light should be unceasing. In the midst of tempests as fierce as those the Church now endures, what would we be without them? If some have gone bad, the good ones shine more brilliantly. (1:132)

I often experience that there is nothing the devils flee from more—without returning—than holy water. They also flee from the cross, but they return. The power of holy water must be great. (1:265)

Let us say the relief [of holy water] is like that coming to a person, very hot and thirsty, on drinking a jar of cold water; it seems the refreshment is felt all over. (1:265)

I consider everything ordained by the Church to be important. (1:265)

I began to beseech His Majesty for the Church. A revelation was given me of the great good that would be done by a religious order in the latter times and of the fortitude with which its members would sustain the faith. (1:359)

The power of holy water must be great. For me there is a particular and very noticeable consolation my soul experiences upon taking it . . . like an interior delight that comforts it entirely. (1:29)

But each order, or, rather, each member must strive that through his instrumentality the Lord might make his order

so prosperous that it will be of service to God in the extreme need the Church is now in. Happy the lives lost for such a purpose! (1:360)

Let those who are to come realize that if the bishop is holy the subjects will be so too; and as something very important always ask this of the Lord in your prayers. (2:52)

I was very happy because for me it is the greatest consolation to see one church more where the Blessed Sacrament is preserved. (3:109)

Behold, these are not the times to believe everyone; believe only those who you see are walking in conformity with Christ's life.... Believe firmly what Holy Mother Church holds, and you can be sure you will be walking along a good path. (2:121)

Now, Lord, now; make the sea calm! May this ship, which is the Church, not always have to journey in a tempest like this. (2:176)

Perhaps we don't know what love is.... It doesn't consist in great delight but in desiring with strong determination to please God in everything, in striving, insofar as possible, not to offend Him, and in asking Him for the advancement of the honor and glory of His Son and the increase of the Catholic Church. These are the signs of love. (2:319)

I submit in everything to what the holy Roman Catholic Church holds, for in this Church I live, declare my faith, and promise to live and die. (2:452)

Nor is it in any way good for persons to complain if they see their order in some decline; rather, they should strive to be the kind of rock on which the edifice may again be raised, for the Lord will help toward that. (3:116)

He who has the keys to bind and loose must be the one to judge. (3:133)

I don't know what trials, however great, should be feared if in exchange something so good comes about for Christianity. (3:187)

Although we often do not take note, it ought to be a great consolation for us that Jesus Christ, true God and true man, is present in the most Blessed Sacrament in many places. (3:187)

This was no small consolation for me, since a blessing coming from a bishop and a saint is something to be highly esteemed. (3:283)

With relaxation there comes sometimes a forgetfulness of what pertains to religious life and its obligations. (3:323)

I could thereby please the Lord in some way. Since we would all be occupied in prayer for those who are the defenders of the Church and for preachers and for learned men who protect her from attack. (2:42)

It is my fear that makes me say this, a fear stemming from the fact that with time, through a lack of carefulness at the beginning, laxity usually creeps into monasteries. (3:338)

This is the reason monasteries and even religious orders have gone so astray in some places. They pay little attention to small matters and hence come to fall in very great ones. (3:344)

So, then, do not think that little help from God is necessary for this great battle these preachers and theologians are fighting; a very great deal is necessary. (2:49)

O college of Christ, where St. Peter, being a fisherman, had more authority—and the Lord wanted it so—than St. Bartholomew, who was a king's son! (2:139)

THE BIBLE

Heaven and earth will pass away, but my words will not pass away.—Matthew 24:35

Learning is a great thing because learned men teach and enlighten us who know little; and, when brought before the truths of Sacred Scripture, we do what we ought. (1:130)

I've always been a friend of men of learning. For though some don't have experience, they don't despise the Spirit nor do they ignore it, because in Sacred Scripture, which they study, they always find the truth of the good spirit. (1:131)

From what I see and know through experience, a locution bears the credentials of being from God if it is in conformity with Sacred Scripture. And if it should deviate from Scripture just a little, I would have incomparably greater assurance that it comes from the devil than I now have that it comes from God, however great this latter assurance may be. (1:218–19)

Truth itself [told] me: ... "All the harm that comes to the world comes from its not knowing the truths of

Scripture in clarity and truth; not one iota of Scripture will fall short." (1:354)

They found that none of my experiences was lacking in conformity with Sacred Scripture. This puts me very much at peace. (1:385)

O Lord, my God, how You possess the words of eternal life, where all mortals will find what they desire if they want to seek it! But what a strange thing, my God, that we forget Your words. (1:450)

For a number of years now the Lord has given me great delight each time I hear or read some words from Solomon's *Song of Songs*. (2:209)

I have always been fond of the words of the Gospels [that have come from that most sacred mouth in the way they were said] and found more recollection in them than in very cleverly written books. (2:118)

One word of His will contain within itself a thousand mysteries, and thus our understanding is only very elementary. (2:210)

The words of Jesus Christ, our King and Lord, cannot fail. (2:436)

FAMILY LIFE

❦

Every sound tree bears good fruit, but the bad tree bears evil fruit.—Matthew 7:17

To have had virtuous and God-fearing parents along with the graces the Lord granted me should have been enough for me to have led a good life. (1:54)

My father was fond of reading good books. . . . These good books together with the care my mother took to have us pray and be devoted to our Lady and to some of the saints began to awaken me. (1:54)

It is a great pity the world is now so unfortunate and blind that it seems to parents their honor lies in not letting the dung of this world's goods be forgotten and in not remembering that sooner or later these things will come to an end. (3:148)

If I should have to give advice, I would tell parents that when their children are this age they ought to be very careful about whom their children associate with. For here lies the root of great evil since our natural bent is toward the worst rather than toward the best. (1:58)

It frightens me sometimes to think of the harm a bad companion can do, and if I hadn't experienced it I wouldn't believe it. Especially during adolescence the harm done must be greater. I should like parents to learn from my experience to be very watchful in this matter.
(1:58–59)

Since worldly honors and recreations are so exalted and one's obligations so poorly understood, may it please God that people do not take for virtue what is sin. . . . There is so much difficulty in getting to know one's obligations that the Lord really needs to intervene in the matter. (1:84)

My fondness for good books was my salvation. (1:63)

I sometimes reflect on the great damage parents do by not striving that their children might always see virtuous deeds of every kind. (1:56–57)

Open the eyes of parents, my God. Make them understand the kind of love they are obliged to have for their children so that they do not do these children so much wrong and are not complained about before God in that final judgement where, even though they may not want to know it, the value of each thing will be understood.
(3:148–49)

O Lord! What a great favor You grant to those children whose parents love them so much as to want them to possess their estates, inheritance, and riches in that blessed life that has no end! (1:148)

They are children more of God than of their parents. (3:152)

The Saints

❦

The virtuous will shine like the sun in the kingdom of their Father.—Matthew 13:43

The world has such a mentality and has so forgotten the great perfection and lofty impulses of love that saints experienced that I think this mentality causes more harm and misfortune in these troubled times we live. (1:234)

Since I felt so lacking in the ways they [the saints] served God, reading about them seemed to benefit and encourage me. (1:261)

It happens to me sometimes that those who I know live there [heaven] are my companions and the ones in whom I find comfort; it seems to me that they are the ones who are truly alive. (1:332)

The teachings of so many saints give me assurance. (1:379)

For with other saints it seems the Lord has given them grace to be of help in one need, whereas with this glorious saint [St. Joseph] I have experience that he helps in all our needs. (1:79)

I took for my advocate and lord the glorious St. Joseph and earnestly recommended myself to him. I saw clearly that as in this need so in other greater ones concerning honor and loss of soul this father and lord of mine came to my rescue in better ways than I knew how to ask for. (1:79)

I don't recall up to this day ever having petitioned [St. Joseph] for anything that he failed to grant. It is an amazing thing the great many favors God has granted me through the mediation of this blessed saint, the dangers I was freed from both of body and soul. (1:79)

The Lord wants us to understand that just as He was subject to St. Joseph on earth—for since bearing the title of father, being the Lord's tutor, Joseph could give the Child command—so in heaven God does whatever he commands. (1:79–80)

Because of my impressive experience of the goods this glorious saint [St. Joseph] obtains from God, I had the desire to persuade all to be devoted to him. (1:80)

I have not known anyone truly devoted to him [St. Joseph] and rendering him special services who has not advanced more in virtue. For in a powerful way he benefits souls who recommend themselves to him. (1:80)

I only ask for the love of God those who do not believe me to try, and they will see through experience the great good that comes from recommending oneself to this glorious patriarch [St. Joseph] and being devoted to him. (1:80)

I was very devoted to the glorious Magdalene and frequently thought about her conversion, especially when I received Communion. . . . I commended myself to this glorious saint that she might obtain pardon for me. (1:101)

The good that one who practices prayer possesses has been written of by many saints and holy persons. (1:96)

O blessed heavenly souls! Help our misery and be our intercessors before the divine mercy that we may be given some of your joy and a share in this clear knowledge you possess. (1:456)

Let us remember our holy fathers of the past. . . . They were as delicate as we. And believe, daughters, that when we begin to conquer these wretched little bodies, we will not be so troubled by them. (2:81)

No wonder the saints, with the help of God, were able to do with the elements whatever they wanted. . . . They had dominion over all worldly things because they labored to take little account of them and were truly subject with all their strength to the Lord of the world. (2:108)

The saints—they can do everything in Christ, as St. Paul said. (2:201)

Please God we will merit to enter heaven; and what is more, to be numbered among those who have advanced so far in the love of God. (2:239)

Life is long, and there are in it many trials, and we need to look at Christ our model, how He suffered them, and also at His apostles and saints, so as to bear these trials with perfection. (2:275–76)

I say, daughters, that we should set our eyes on Christ, our Good, and on His saints. There we shall learn true humility, the intellect will be enhanced, as I have said, and self-knowledge will not make one base and cowardly.
(2:293)

Look at the multitude of souls God draws to Himself by means of one. He is to be greatly praised for the thousands converted by the martyrs: for a young girl like St. Ursula; for those the devil must have lost through St. Dominic, St. Francis, and other founders of religious orders. (2:356)

For if here below, as David says, in the company of the saints we will become saints, there is no reason to doubt that, being united with the Strong One through so sovereign a union of spirit with spirit, fortitude will cling to such a soul; and so we shall understand what fortitude the saints had. (2:447–48)

I am not surprised that this seemed madness to them, since nowadays the world is very rooted in discretion and has almost forgotten the great favors God granted to the many holy men and women who served Him in the desert. (3:258)

How many saints we have in heaven.... Let us adopt the holy presumption that with the Lord's help we will be like them. The battle will be brief, my Sisters, and the end is eternal. (3:279–80)